Genre Read-Aloud
Anthology

Mc
Graw
Hill
Education

mhreadingwonders.com

Send all inquiries to:
McGraw-Hill Education
2 Penn Plaza
New York, NY 10121

ISBN: 978-0-07-898219-4
MHID: 0-07-898219-7

Printed in the United States of America.

3 4 5 6 7 QVS 22 21 20 19 18

A

CONTENTS

`Fiction`

Informational Text

READ-ALOUDS: AN IMPORTANT COMPONENT OF BALANCED LITERACY

by Kathy Rhea Bumgardner, MEd
National Literacy Consultant
North Carolina Educator Strategies Unlimited, Inc. Belmont, North Carolina
Creator of Think Aloud Clouds and Literacy Toolkits for Comprehension
Professional Development Videos for Instructional Best Practices in Literacy

DGLimages/Shutterstock.com

Introduction

The read-aloud is a strategic instructional practice in which the teacher sets aside time to read texts orally to students on a consistent basis from selected various texts. The lessons are interactive and deepen students' understanding of the text through text-dependent questions.

How important is it that teachers read aloud to their students on a daily basis? How can we ensure that, with so much to accomplish in today's 21st century classrooms, the benefits of reading aloud are worth the instructional time spent in class?

Books play an important role in students' academic and social development.

Reading high-quality books increases students' overall language competence, and the process of reading, listening, questioning, and responding to a story provides a foundation for reflective and critical thinking (Pressley, 2006). Children imitate their teachers, and they are eager to read the books their teachers read (Cunningham, 2005).

The Value of the Read-Aloud

The read-aloud in today's classrooms should be a valuable and intentional part of good instruction. It can be a highly effective strategy for nurturing and developing literacy learners. It can be that match to light that love of reading fire for students.

In 1985 the report of the Commission on Reading, *Becoming a Nation of Readers*, made a lasting statement about reading aloud (p. 23). They stated: "The single most important activity for building the knowledge required for eventual success in reading is read aloud to children" (1985).

Read-alouds allow children to access more complex text than they can access while reading on their own, as well as access more complex concepts.

In the absence of the read-alouds, we may slow students' vocabulary learning; research has shown a strong positive correlation between read-aloud experiences and vocabulary development (Meehan, 1999; Roberts, 2008; Sénéchal & LeFevre, 2002; Sharif, Ozuah, Dinkevich, & Mulvihill, 2003). A well-planned read-aloud can repeatedly expose children to academic vocabulary that will likely show up in content textbooks.

Teachers can use read-alouds to increase their students' comprehension skills, foster their critical thinking through discussion and demonstration, and develop their students' background knowledge and interest in quality literature. While reading, teachers can model oral reading fluency and encourage strategies that students can implement during independent reading.

Preparing for Successful Read-Alouds

Choosing short, high quality and high interest texts is the important first step for an interactive read-aloud lesson. These texts should be complex due to structure, the use of language conventions, background knowledge, and/or levels of meaning. Providing interaction with a variety of texts is key.

High interest informational texts should be included. When Nell Duke (2000) examined the use of informational texts in 20 first-grade classrooms, she found that on average, children spent 3.6 minutes a day on informational texts, with urban schools spending 1.9 minutes a day. With the recent emphasis on a shift towards increasing informational texts, it is important to consider that balance of the genres is crucial. Encounters with high interest informational texts, as well as high quality narrative read-alouds, give depth to the read-aloud.

ILeysen/Shutterstock.com

In order to deliver an effective read-aloud, teachers should maintain a productive quality to the pacing, tone, and setting of read-aloud time to establish healthy expectations while optimizing learning potential. Teachers should consider structuring the read-aloud around skill building as much as for enjoyment (Layne, 2015).

Setting the stage for a read-aloud by including and modeling think-alouds can provide crucial scaffolding for students. The think-aloud strategy helps teachers to intentionally demonstrate for readers how to think about how they make meaning (Beers, 2003).

Strategic think alouds during the read-aloud are a way of making public the thinking that goes on inside your head as you read.

Reading aloud is still an essential tool to not only motivate readers to enjoy reading but also to assist in helping students on their academic journey to be college and career ready.

A Great Resource for Genre Focus

One of the most valuable things a teacher can do to support early readers with understanding various genres is to use read-alouds. Teachers will find that strategic read-alouds are a valuable resource for helping students to navigate their work in multiple genres.

For example, if students are reading fiction, the richness of a read-aloud can help them with key reading skills and strategies such as asking and answering questions, with a focus on characters, settings, and the major events of a story. The read-aloud time can also provide students with opportunities to have accountable collaborative conversations with their peers and teachers about the elements and deepen their comprehension.

In informational texts, the focus should be on facts and key details about the topic. This includes the importance of vocabulary and the author's sequencing of information. Through read-alouds, the students will be interactively engaged and guided to listen for those important key details.

Listening and reading for key details in fiction and informational texts are two different actions. Read-alouds can provide the teacher a consistent and strategic opportunity to allow students to both hear and discuss those key details while learning how to listen differently for, and gaining comprehension with, each genre.

The read-aloud and follow-up conversation allows teachers the opportunity to help students develop background knowledge and connect concepts so that all children can begin to clarify their thinking during their discussions with their peers and teacher (Dorn & Soffos, 2005).

Next steps:

- Pre-read and reread the selection to determine what part of the text you will read.
- Consider your reading goals and focus.
- Identify the process and strategy information (at work in the text).
- Anticipate where background knowledge needs to be built.
- Highlight places to stop for the think alouds where you can question or make meaningful connections.
- Plan for possible discussion questions before the lesson.
- Practice reading the selection using gestures and voice intonation.
- Plan for possible discussion questions before the lesson.

References

Cunningham, P. (2005). Struggling readers: "If they don't read much, how they ever gonna get good?" The Reading Teacher 59 (1): 88–90.

Pressley, M. (2006). Reading instruction that works: The case for balanced teaching, 3rd ed. New York: Guilford.

Trelease, J., & Trelease, J. (2013) The Read-Aloud Handbook- 7th Ed. New York, NY: Penquin Books.

Richard C. Anderson, Elfrieda H. Hiebert, Judith A. Scott, and Ian A. G. Wilkinson, Becoming a Nation of Readers: The Report of the Commission on Reading, U. S. Department of Education (Champaign-Urbana, IL: Center for the Study of Reading, 1985), p. 23.

Layne, S. (2015) In defense of read aloud-sustaining best practice. Stenhouse Publishers (town?)

Beers, K. (2003). When kids can't read, what teachers can do. Portsmouth, NH: Heinemann, p. 101.

Duke, N. K. (2000). 3.6 minutes per day: The scarcity of informational texts in first grade. Reading Research Quarterly, 35(2), 202–224.

Meehan, M. L. (1999). Evaluation of the Monomgalia County schools' Even Start program child vocabulary outcomes. Charleston, WV: AEL.

Roberts, T. (2008). Home storybook reading in primary or second language preschool children: Evidence of equal effectiveness for second language vocabulary acquisition. Reading Research Quarterly, 43(2), 103–130.

Sénéchal, M., & LeFevre, J. A. (2002). Parental involvement in the development of children's reading skill: A five year longitudinal study. Child Development, 73(2), 445–460.

Sharif, I., Ozuah, P. O., Dinkevich, E. I., & Mulvihill, M. (2003). Impact of a brief literacy intervention on urban preschoolers. Early Childhood Education Journal, 30(3), 177–180.

Dorn, L., & Soffos, C. (2005). Teaching for deep comprehension. Portland, ME: Stenhouse.

HOW TO USE THE GENRE READ–ALOUD ANTHOLOGY

Key Features of the Genre Read–Aloud Anthology

- The selections in this anthology feature engaging read–aloud experiences in a variety of genres.

- The selections in the book are grouped together by genres.

- Each selection includes 2–4 color images that can be shown while reading.

- The selections include instructional prompts at point-of-use:
  - Genre feature box that focuses on an aspect of the genre
  - Think-alouds demonstrating how to use comprehension skills and strategies with the stories
  - Questions that focus on genre features
  - Questions about the text
  - Oral vocabulary words that have been highlighted in the text with child-friendly definitions

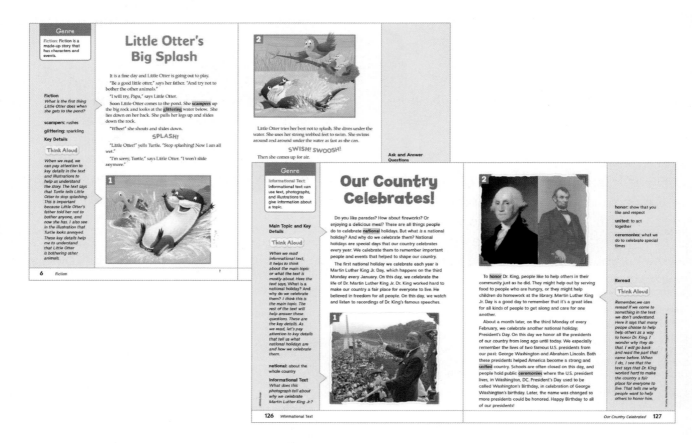

Tips for Using the Genre Read–Aloud Anthology

Choose a Story

This anthology has been designed for flexible use. The stories are organized by genre, so pick one to enhance your genre focus. You can also find stories that support themes, incorporate skills and strategies, and other instructional goals.

Preview the Story

Reading the story ahead of time will help you to anticipate background knowledge gaps. It will also help you decide where to pause for emphasis and where to elicit questions, predictions, or reactions. You may even want to practice reading it aloud.

Preview the Instructional Prompts

Preview the sidebar prompts to think about when you want to use them.

Read with Expression

Let your voice reflect the tone of the story or the personalities of the characters. Don't read too fast. Vary your pace so you can pause for emphasis. Allow time for children to think about what's happening or what might come next.

Model Your Own Engagement

Model your own reading process, focusing on language patterns or phrases you liked or parts of the text that made you feel or visualize something. Talk about what you notice. Model using the vocabulary words.

Encourage Children to Participate

Allow time for children to look at the pictures, make comments, and ask questions. Invite them to make predictions and share ideas about how the characters changed, or to talk about new information presented. Encourage them to use the vocabulary words.

Reread

Rereading the selection is recommended. Rereading is a good opportunity to focus on instruction, to ask questions about comprehension, and to clarify aspects of the text that may be confusing. You may also choose passages to reread that require more attention.

Key Details

Think Aloud

When we read, we pay attention to details to understand the story better. In this part of the story, Bird and Squirrel try to stand on one leg and clap. I look at the illustration and see that they are smiling. These details tell me that they like being able to do the same thing. Let's pay attention to details as the story continues.

Bird and Squirrel

One day Bird was all alone in the **meadow** when he saw a squirrel.

"Hello," said Bird. "Let's play."

He stood on one leg and clapped three times.

"You try!" he said.

Squirrel stood on one leg and clapped three times.

"Hooray!" said Bird.

"Hooray!" said Squirrel.

"Try this," said Squirrel.

She closed her eyes and counted by twos.

"2-4-6-8-10," she said.

"Oh, let me try!" said Bird. "2-4-6-8 . . . Umm."

"10!" said Squirrel.

"10!" Bird repeated.

"Hooray!" said Squirrel.

"Hooray!" said Bird.

"Try this!" said Bird. He opened his beak wide and whistled.

Tweet Tweet Toot Toot Tweet Tweet

Squirrel opened her mouth. She **puckered** her lips and blew out air. But there was no sound.

"No," said Bird. "Not like that. Like this!"

Tweet Tweet Toot Toot Tweet Tweet

Squirrel opened her mouth, puckered her lips, and blew out as hard as she could.

But no matter how hard she tried, she couldn't whistle.

Bird whistled even louder.

TOOT TOOT! TWEET TWEET!

"Hooray!" he cried.

Squirrel didn't say anything.

Then Squirrel crouched down on her hind legs. She **sprang** up into the air and flipped her tail over her head.

She landed on one foot.

"You try," she said to Bird.

puckered: scrunched up

Ask and Answer Questions

Think Aloud

As we read, we ask ourselves questions to help us understand the story. I read that Bird can whistle and Squirrel can't. I ask myself how Squirrel feels about this. I look for clues in the text. I read that Squirrel doesn't say anything when Bird says, "Hooray!" I think this might mean she feels bad.

sprang: jumped

Key Details

Look at the illustrations. How does Bird feel about not being able to flip over? How can you tell?

Bird crouched down low and then sprang up. He tried to flip over. But he landed on his head.

"Ouch!" said Bird.

"Not like that," said Squirrel. "Like this!"

She sprang into the air and flipped over. This time she landed on the other foot.

"Hooray!" she cried.

Bird didn't say anything.

Bird looked at Squirrel.

Squirrel looked at Bird.

They both looked away.

Then Bird had an idea. He started to whistle quietly.

tweet tweet toot toot tweet tweet

Squirrel began to move **gracefully** from side to side.

gracefully: easily and smoothly

Bird whistled faster.

Tweet Toot! Tweet Toot! Tweet Toot!

Squirrel sprang into the air.

TOOT! TOOT! TOOT!

Bird whistled louder than before.

Squirrel flipped over.

TW - E - E - E - E - T !

Bird held the note as long as he could.

Squirrel landed and took a bow.

"Hooray!" cried Bird.

"Hooray!" cried Squirrel.

"Let's do it again!" they both said at **exactly** the same time.

And that is just what they did. For the rest of that day and the next day and for a long time to come.

exactly: the same as

Ask and Answer Questions:
What questions do you have about how Bird and Squirrel act at the end of the story?

Fiction

What is the first thing Little Otter does when she gets to the pond?

scampers: rushes

glittering: sparkling

Key Details

Think Aloud

When we read, we can pay attention to key details in the text and illustrations to help us understand the story. The text says that Turtle tells Little Otter to stop splashing. This is important because Little Otter's father told her not to bother anyone, and now she has. I also see in the illustration that Turtle looks annoyed. These key details help me to understand that Little Otter is bothering other animals.

Little Otter's Big Splash

It is a fine day and Little Otter is going out to play.

"Be a good little otter," says her father. "And try not to bother the other animals."

"I will try, Papa," says Little Otter.

Soon Little Otter comes to the pond. She **scampers** up the big rock and looks at the **glittering** water below. She lies down on her back. She pulls her legs up and slides down the rock.

"Whee!" she shouts and slides down.

SPLASH!

"Little Otter!" yells Turtle. "Stop splashing! Now I am all wet."

"I'm sorry, Turtle," says Little Otter. "I won't slide anymore."

Little Otter tries her best not to splash. She dives under the water. She uses her strong webbed feet to swim. She swims around and around under the water as fast as she can.

SWISH! SWOOSH!

Then she comes up for air.

"Little Otter!" cries Frog. "Be careful! You made so many waves that I fell off my lily pad!"

"I'm sorry, Frog," says Little Otter. "I won't swim underwater anymore."

Little Otter comes to a log. She pushes it with her front paws. She kicks and kicks.

SPLISH! SPLASH!

"Beep! Beep!" she cries out. "Taxi! Who wants to ride in my taxi?"

"Little Otter, stop that splashing," says a voice. "My babies are getting wet."

Little Otter looks up. She sees a mother bird and three tiny birds inside a nest.

"I'm sorry, Mama Bird," says Little Otter. "I won't play taxi anymore."

Ask and Answer Questions

Think Aloud

As we read, it helps to ask ourselves questions to help understand the text better. I read that someone asks Little Otter to stop splashing. I ask myself why someone would do that. Then I read on and learn that it was a Mama Bird and Little Otter is getting her babies wet. That makes sense. Now I ask myself how Little Otter will feel about that.

cause: make happen

Key Details

Listen to the words of Little Otter's song. Look at the illustration of her singing. How is she feeling? What details tell you that she is feeling this way?

Little Otter sits on the rock. She thinks about what Papa Otter told her. "There is nothing I can do that won't **cause** trouble," she sighs. She makes up a sad song.

> **Slide! Splash!**
> **No, Little Otter, don't do that!**
> **Dive! Swim!**
> **No, Little Otter that's not good either.**
> **Oh, what can a Little Otter do-ooh-ooh?**
> **Oh, what can a Little Otter do?**

When suddenly she hears:

Splash!

"Little Otter!" cries Turtle. "I asked you not to splash."
"I'm sorry, Turtle," says Little Otter.
Then she realizes that she DIDN'T splash. Who did?
"Help!" comes a voice. It is Mama Bird. "My baby fell in. Someone please save him!"
Little Otter slides down the rock.

SPLASH!

She dives under the water and swims fast with her strong webbed feet.

SWISH! SWISH!

She comes to the log and pushes it with her front paws. She kicks as hard as she can.

SPLISH! SPLASH!

"Beep! Beep!" she calls. "Taxi coming through!"

She comes to the baby bird. She pick him up **gently** and puts him on top of the log. Then she kicks the log to the **shore**. The baby bird is safe.

"Hooray for Little Otter!" shout the other animals.

Little Otter smiles. "It is what a Little Otter can do," she says. Then she and dives into the water.

"Have fun, Little Otter!" says Mama Bird.

"Yes," say the other animals.

SPLASH!!

Little Otter kicks and laughs. It is her biggest and best splash ever.

gently: softly and with care

shore: land right next water

Ask and Answer Questions

What questions do you have about how Little Otter feels at the end of the story? What questions do you have about how the other animals feel about Little Otter now?

Fiction

Fiction has a setting. Where does this story take place?

constructed: made

Key Details

Think Aloud

As we read, it helps to pay attention to key details in the text and pictures. Here Jack tells Beep to follow the rules. I notice that Beep says, "Rules?" and shakes his head. I think this means that Beep doesn't even know what the word rules means. Why is this detail important? I will pay attention to more details as I continue to read.

Beep Follows the Rules

One rainy afternoon, Tanya and her little brother Jack got tired of playing checkers. So they went down into the basement and built a robot. He was small and cute, with a toaster for a body, a clock for a head, and egg carton eyes. They **constructed** arms and legs out of old spoons.

Beep! Beep! Beep! said the robot.

"Let's call him Beep!" said Jack.

"Let's play tag," said Tanya. "You're IT."

Then Jack ran and Tanya chased him.

Beep! Beep! Beep! said Beep.

Beep chased Jack. Beep was fast and tagged him.

Beeeep! Beeeep!

"Hey!" said Jack. "Tanya is IT. You can't tag me. You're not following the rules!"

"Rules?" asked Beep, shaking his head.

"Never mind," said Tanya. "Let's build a fort."

They tiptoed to Jack's room as quietly as they could because the baby was sleeping.

Tanya began building.

"Beep, can you get some pillows?" she asked, pointing to the bed.

Beep climbed up on the bed. Then he started jumping!

Beepity! Beepity! Beepity! BEEP!

"Hey!" said Jack. "No jumping on the bed! It's a rule."

"Rule?" asked Beep, hanging his head.

"Never mind," said Tanya. "Let's get a snack. I wonder what robots like to eat?"

She found out soon enough, because when they got to the kitchen, Beep was already there, with an empty cookie jar. He really was fast.

"Beep!" said Jack. "We are **permitted** only one treat after school. It's a rule!"

Visualize

Think Aloud

Visualizing what happens in the story helps us understand the text better. I think about the author's words. Then I create a picture in my mind. Here the author says that Beep hangs his head when Jack tells him not to jump on the bed. When I picture Beep hanging his head, it seems as if he feels sad. Why do you think Beep feels sad?

permitted: allowed

3

Key Details

Beep ate all the treats! Now Tanya wants to do something quiet such as read a book. Why do you think she suggests that?

Beep Crunch Beep! Beep Crunch Beep!

"Beep, you're not following the rules!" said Tanya.

"Rules?" asked Beep, looking **puzzled**.

Tanya and Jack shook their heads in **dismay**.

"Maybe we should do something quiet, like read a book," said Tanya.

Jack picked a joke book. "You'll like this, Beep," he said.

And Beep did like the book. A lot.

Beep! Beep! Beep! Beep! Beep!

"I think he's laughing!" said Jack. "Shh!!" said Tanya. "The baby is sleeping. No loud noises during nap time. It's a rule." But it was too late.

WAAAH!! WAAAH!!

"Oh, no," said Tanya. "Now we're in trouble."

A few seconds later Dad walked in. "What's going on in here?" he said.

"Sorry, Dad," said Tanya. "It's just that our robot doesn't know how to follow the rules."

"Your Robot!?" Dad asked. Jack pointed at Beep.

"Wow," said Dad. "Did you tell this robot the rules?"

"Beep, do you KNOW the rules?" asked Jack.

Beep shook his whole clock radio head.

"Let's make a list," said Tanya. "Rules for Robots. No jumping on the bed!"

"One treat after school!" said Jack.

"We can add more when we think of them," said Tanya

Beep loved his list. It turned out that robots are very good at following the rules. Once they know them. In fact Beep was SO good at following the rules hat he made sure to **scold** Jack and Tanya if THEY ever got a little loud.

BEEP BEEP BEEP BEEP BEEP

or tried to sneak a treat . . .

BEEP BEEP BEEP BEEP BEEP

"Sometimes Beep sounds just like my old alarm clock," said Tanya, covering her ears.

"He IS your old alarm clock," said Jack.

"Oh yeah," said Tanya. "Well, it's a good thing he's so much fun to play with!"

"Let's play tag!" said Jack.

And Beep knew just what to do.

scold: tell someone what they are doing is wrong.

Visualize

What do you picture in your mind when Beep says "Beep Beep Beep" each time Jack and Tanya break a rule. Why do you think he does that?

Rules for Robots
No jumping on the bed
One treat after school
Be quiet at naptime

Genre

Fiction: Fiction is a made-up story with events that happen in a certain order, or sequence.

Fiction

Fiction has events that happen order. What is the first thing to happen in this story?

Key Details

Think Aloud

As we read, it helps to pay attention to key details in the words and illustrations. Lila tells her father it is dark and that she will be all alone. This makes me think that she is worried and could get upset when he leaves. What makes this a key detail? Let's continue to pay attention to key details as we read.

companion: someone to be with

clutches: holds tightly

The Night is Talking

"It is bedtime," says Daddy. "Close your eyes and try to sleep."

"But it's dark when I close my eyes," says Lila. "And I will be all alone."

"Teddy will be your **companion**," says Daddy. "And I will be right outside your door."

Lila holds Teddy to her ear.

"Teddy doesn't want to sleep yet," she says.

"Shh . . ." says Daddy. "You and Teddy need to be still and close your eyes. Tomorrow will come soon."

He tucks Lila in, gives her a good-night kiss, and tiptoes out.

Lila **clutches** Teddy and closes her eyes.

But...

Tick, Tock

The clock on her night table is talking.

Purr, Purr

The cat lying on her bed is talking.

Beep, Beep

The cars outside are talking.

Squeak, Squeak

The floors above her are talking.

Bark, Bark

The dog next door is talking.

Rumble, Roar

The thunder in the sky is talking.

Visualize

Think Aloud

As we read, it helps to visualize what the words are saying. This means to use the words to form a picture in your mind. Here, I read about sounds that Lila is hearing while lying in bed. I can visualize a room with a clock ticking and a cat purring. I can visualize that she lives on a busy street with horns beeping. I can picture that there is a storm outside. All of this helps me to understand where Lila is and how she is feeling about the noise around her.

Visualize

What do you think Lila's expression is like when she calls her father? How do you picture her? How does this help you understand the story?

fretting: worrying

stir: move

peep: make a sound

"Daddy!" calls Lila.

Daddy enters. "Why are you **fretting**?" he asks.

"The night is talking and I can't sleep," says Lila. "Please, tell it to be quiet."

Daddy listens to the night talking.

Then he sits beside Lila and begins to sing.

Tick, tock
Be quiet clock.
It is time to sleep.

Purr, purr
*Cat, don't **stir**.*
Lila needs to sleep.

Beep, beep
*Horn, don't **peep**.*
Let little Lila sleep.

Squeak, squeak
Floor, don't speak.
Night time is for sleep.

Bark, bark
Dog, it is dark.
My darling needs to sleep.

Rumble, roar
Thunder, no more.
It is time for sleep.

ZZZZZ-ZZZZZ

What is that sound?
It is Lila talking—while she is fast asleep!

Key Details
At the end of the story, it is Lila who is making a sound. What is this sound? Why is this detail important?

Genre

Fiction: Fiction often has illustrations that help tell the story.

Character, Setting, and Events

Think Aloud

When we read fiction, it helps to pay attention to what the characters do. So far, this story is about a baby pig named Chester. His brothers and sister think he is too little to go with them. But when they take him out, Chester says "Whee!" and waves. This tells me that he knows what is happening. Maybe he isn't such a baby after all. Let's look for more things Chester does as we read.

capable: can do a lot

Fiction

What does the illustration tell you about Chester? How does it help you understand the story better?

Chester's Day Out

The three little piglets were getting ready to go out.

"Today," said Mama Pig. "You will take your baby brother with you."

"But Chester is too little," complained his big brothers and sister. "He can't do anything."

"Nonsense," said Mama Pig. "Chester is a very **capable** baby pig. I am sure he will surprise you."

She dressed Chester in his new outfit and placed him in a bright red wagon.

"Whee!" said Chester excitedly.

He waved at his mother as his brothers and sister took turns pulling him along.

2

First the piglets stopped at the playground, just like always.

"You stay in the wagon," they said to Chester.

And they ran off to play ball with the skunks.

The piglets kicked and ran and caught the ball. Soon, the game was tied. Then the skunks kicked and the ball flew high up in the sky. The ball flew past the sandboxes and swings. It flew all the way to Chester.

"Look out, Chester!" called his brothers and sister.

"Wheeee!" shouted Chester. He stood up and waved his arms. Down came the ball. Right in his arms!

"The piglets are the winners!" announced the coach. "What an **athlete**!" she added and then put a huge trophy in Chester's wagon. "Bring him back anytime."

Chester's brothers and sister looked at Chester and looked at the trophy and shook their heads.

Visualize

> **Think Aloud**

As I read, I try to visualize what is happening in the text. To do this I listen to the words and make a picture in my mind. Chester's brothers and sister shake their heads when they look at his trophy. I picture people I know shaking their heads like that and I can see the way they look. This tells me that they are surprised about Chester and his trophy.

athlete: someone who plays sports

Next, the piglets went to the library, just like always. They left Chester near the picture books and ran off to their favorite sections.

"Can I help you find a book?" the librarian asked Chester.

Chester stood up in the wagon and pointed.

"Want!" he said

"*Peter Rabbit.* Excellent choice!" said the librarian. He pulled the book down and put it in the wagon.

Chester pointed to several more books.

"Want!" he said. And soon the librarian had filled his wagon with all kinds of books.

"Your baby brother certainly loves books," said the librarian. "What a reader! Bring him back anytime."

Next, it was time to do the shopping. The piglets went to the grocery store, just like always.

"You stay here," his brothers and sister said to Chester. Then they ran off to find the food that Mama had asked them to get.

Chester rolled down the aisle and stopped in the fruit section.

Character, Setting, and Events

What happens to Chester at the library? How is it similar to what happened at the playground?

"Whee!" he said. He pushed a shiny apple into a passing shopping cart.

"What a delicious looking apple," said the **customer**. "Thank you!"

Chester did this several more times and soon there were no apples left. The store owner was **thrilled** that customers were buying so many apples.

"What a salesperson!" she said. She gave Chester a giant basket of fruit as a **reward**. "Bring him back anytime."

His brothers and sister put the fruit basket in the cart next to the picture books and the trophy. They each took turns pulling Chester back home. Mama was there to greet them.

"Whee!" said Chester. He waved his arms and his mama picked him up.

"What a capable baby pig!" said his mama, looking at all of the things in his wagon.

And his brothers and sister had to agree.

customer: a shopper

thrilled: excited and happy

reward: a prize or present for doing something well

Visualize

How do you think Chester's wagon looks when he gets home? What is in it? What does this tell his mama about his day out?

Ask and Answer Questions

Think Aloud

We can ask ourselves questions if we do not understand something we read. The text says that Rockwell wants to be a superhero and rescue people. I wonder how a little boy can really do that. Will Rockwell do things like a real superhero or will he be like a real boy? As I read on, I will try to answer this question.

assistant: helper

announced: said loudly

Rockwell to the Rescue!

One day, Rockwell decided to become a superhero. He asked his mom for an old sheet. He made it into a cape. He folded red construction paper to make a hat.

Then he put a matching red bandana on his dog, Rex, who would become his super **assistant.**

"Rockwell and Rex to the rescue!" he **announced** as they came into the kitchen.

"Who will you rescue?" asked Rockwell's dad.

"Whoever needs it," said Rockwell.

"Great!" said Dad, grabbing his coat. "We can start right here in the neighborhood."

Rockwell didn't know who he could rescue in his very own neighborhood, but he went anyway.

Rockwell and Rex and Dad turned the corner.

"Rockwell and Rex to the rescue!" Rockwell shouted.

He looked up in the tree in case a cat was stuck there. Then he could rescue it.

Instead he heard crying.

"Wah! Wah!" It was Daniel, the little boy who lived next door.

Daniel's mom was bent over the stroller, **comforting** him.

"Doggie!" Daniel called as soon as he saw Rex. Daniel loved Rex. He stopped crying. He looked up at Rockwell and Rex.

"Peek-a-boo!" said Rockwell. Daniel started to laugh.

"Thank you, Rockwell and Rex," said Daniel's mom. "I don't know what I would have done without you."

Rockwell and Rex and Dad waved goodbye and walked some more.

comforting: making someone feel better

Character, Setting, Events

Think Aloud

Let's think about the characters, the setting, and the events. Rockwell is the main character. He is a little boy who wants to be a superhero. He is in his neighborhood. That is the setting. Rockwell is making a crying little boy laugh. That is an event. Let's look for more events as we read.

"Rockwell and Rex to the rescue!" Rockwell cried out as they walked down the street.

He looked under a car, just in case someone was stuck there. Instead he saw something shiny. It was keys.

"Dad, look!" said Rockwell. "Someone lost their keys."

Just then, Mr. and Mrs. Kim passed by. Mrs. Kim was carrying Fiddles the cat.   Mr. Kim had lots of packages. He was looking at the ground.

"Rockwell found these keys," said Dad.

"Thank you, Rockwell," said Mrs. Kim. "We were just looking for those!"

Rockwell and Dad helped Mr. Kim with his packages. Mrs. Kim gave them homemade muffins and let Rockwell pet Fiddles.

Rockwell and Rex and Dad said goodbye and continued their walk. They passed the playground. There was a new boy just trying to get on a swing.

"Rockwell and Rex to the rescue!" Rockwell called out.

Realistic Fiction:

What parts of this story could happen in real life? Are there any parts that could not happen in real life?

"I can hold the swing while you get on," Rockwell told the boy.

"Thank you," said the boy. "My name is Ryan and I just moved here."

"I am Rockwell and this is Rex," said Rockwell. "We are superheroes."

"I love playing superheroes," said Ryan.

"Let's play together soon!" said Rockwell.

Rockwell and Rex and Dad walked home.

That night, Rockwell took off his cape and hat. He took off Rex's bandana. They got ready for bed.

"You had a **successful** first day as a superhero," said Dad.

But there wasn't anyone to rescue!" said Rockwell.

"Nonsense," said Dad. "What would your neighbors have done without your **support** today?"

Rockwell thought about Daniel and Mr. and Mrs. Kim and Ryan. He smiled. He could be a superhero for his neighbors! He closed his eyes to get some sleep. He would need all his energy to rescue more neighbors tomorrow.

Charater, Setting, Events
Where is Rockwell now? Who is he talking to? What does he do?

successful: did a good job

support: help

Ask and Answer Questions
What questions do you have about how Rockwell acted like a superhero?

Genre

Realistic Fiction: Realistic fiction has characters that can be found in real life.

Jacob's Beanstalk

One day, Jacob's teacher read a story called "Jack and the Beanstalk." In it, a boy named Jack planted a seed that grew overnight into a huge beanstalk. Jack climbed up, Up, UP beyond the clouds, to a castle where a giant lived.

It was the best story Jacob had ever heard.

On the bus ride home, all Jacob could think about was having his very own magic beanstalk.

"Do you think a plant can really grow up to the sky like that?" he asked his friend, Claudio.

"If the seed is really a magic seed," said Claudio.

"There's no such thing as a plant that grows up, Up, UP to the sky," said the other kids.

"I think there is," said Jacob.

When he got home, Jacob asked his mom for a magic seed so he could grow a beanstalk and meet a giant.

"I don't know of any seeds with *that* kind of magic," his mom said. "But all seeds have a little magic." She handed Jacob a packet of seeds.

Character, Setting, Events

Think Aloud

When we read, it helps to think about what the characters say and do. Jacob loves the story, "Jack and the Beanstalk." He wants to grow a plant just like Jack's. This help me to understand that Jacob is a character who has a lot of imagination. Let's look for other things that Jacob says and does that tell what he is like.

First, he found a spot in the garden big enough for a beanstalk. He dug into the earth and then added dark, rich soil. He **poked** one hole, neat and round, and dropped the largest seed into the ground. Then he covered it with soil. He couldn't wait for his special seed to grow to the sky.

When the sun rose the next day, Jacob **peeked** out his window. His eyes traveled up, up, up, beyond the clouds. But, where was his beanstalk?

He rushed to the garden. No stem. No leaf. No beanstalk.

"My seed isn't a special seed after all," Jacob told his dad.

"Seeds need time to grow," his dad said.

At school, Jacob told the kids about planting a beanstalk.

"That seed will never grow up, Up, UP," said Mason.

"Even a magic seed needs time to grow," said Jacob.

After school, Jacob headed straight to the garden.

No stem. No leaf. No beanstalk. No matter, he thought.

Seeds need time and water to grow. Jacob tipped the pail and watched the water spill like silver drops into the earth.

poked: make a hole

peeked: looked at for a second

Reread

Think Aloud

If we don't understand something, it can help to reread what came before. Here, Jacob says his seed isn't a special seed after all. I wonder why he is saying that. I will reread what came before to find out. I see that the text says, "He couldn't wait for his special seed to grow to the sky." But there is no beankstalk yet. That is why his seed isn't special.

Realistic Fiction

What is Jacob doing in the picture? How is he acting like a real child?

headed to: went

pesky: annoying

concerned: worried

The sun warmed the ground, the water soaked the seed, and Jacob waited for something to happen.

When he **headed to** the garden the next day, Jacob expected to see something big and wonderful.

Instead? No stem. No leaf. No beanstalk.

"What are you doing?" his sister asked.

Jacob smoothed the soil and pulled the **pesky** weeds. "Just looking," he said.

His sister shook her head. "That bean will never grow up to the sky."

"Seeds need time to grow," said Jacob.

The sun warmed the earth, the water soaked the seed. When Jacob had finished pulling the last weed, he sat down to wait. He imagined he was Jack, climbing up Up, UP, beyond the clouds.

Every day for many days, Jacob took care of his seed, watering and weeding and waiting. Everyone at school kept saying that his seed would never make a beanstalk. But Jacob wasn't **concerned**.

After more days of waiting, Jacob wondered, what would Jack do? Finally, he knew. He bent low and whispered the magic words:

Little seed,
asleep below,
don't be afraid.
It's time to grow!

When Jacob woke early the next morning, he didn't need to look out the window to know that something BIG, amazing, and wonderful had happened.

Just as he knew it would, a tiny sprout with green leaves pushed through the soil. A beanstalk! It might not have gone Up, Up, UP all the way to the sky. And there was probably not going to be a giant either. But it was his beanstalk and it had grown from a tiny seed and it felt just like magic.

Reread
Why does Jacob think something wonderful has happened? Let's reread the parts that came before to find out.

Character, Setting, Events
What happens at the end of the story? Why does Jacob feel it's like magic?

4

Plot: Sequence

Think Aloud

When we read, it helps to pay attention to the sequence, or the order in which things happen. Words such as first, next, *and* last *help us to know the order. Suchan is trying to figure out what snow is. The text says, "First, he goes to his big sister." This tells me that he will ask his sister first. Let's look for what Suchan does next to figure out what snow is.*

crystals: something small that has many sides and can usually be seen through

Suchan's First Snow

Suchan came from a faraway place to live with his new family. He loves his new home and school. But today school is closed because it is going to snow!

Suchan has never seen snow before. He is very curious.

First, he goes to his big sister, Elena, who is looking out the window.

"What is snow?" he asks.

"Snow is like winter fairies dancing in the sky," says his sister.

Suchan thinks about that. He's never seen a fairy before but he likes to dance.

Next, Suchan finds his dad in the kitchen reading.

"What is snow?" he asks his dad.

"Snow is science," Dad says. "Water in the clouds freezes. That makes ice **crystals**. Then the ice crystals fall to the ground as snowflakes."

Suchan thinks about that. He's never seen crystals before but he has tasted ice.

Then, he waits outside for the snow. Mr. Hill, the mail carrier, comes up the sidewalk.

"Hello, Suchan!" he says. "Are you excited about the snow?"

Suchan nods but asks, "What is snow, Mr. Hill?"

"Snow is slipping and sliding," Mr. Hill says. "Very tricky stuff so I have to **deliver** my mail early. Goodbye!"

Suchan thinks about that. Slipping and sliding sounds fun. And he likes tricks.

Suchan brings the mail inside.

"Mom," he asks. "What is snow?"

Mom **places** a cup of cocoa in front of him. "Snow is winter magic that builds **memories**," she says.

Suchan thinks about that as he sips his cocoa. He likes to build things.

deliver: bring to

places: puts

memories: things you remember

Realistic Fiction
Who is Suchan talking to? What are they talking about? Why is this important to the story?

Visualize

Think Aloud

When we read it helps to visualize what the text is saying. To do this you make a picture in your mind. The text says that Suchan is sipping cocoa and thinking. I visualize him smiling to himself thinking about all of the things he could build.

Suchan drinks the last sip of cocoa and goes to the window.

"It's snowing!" he yells.

Goldie the dog runs to him. They watch the snow together.

Suchan's big sister comes in. "It's **chilly** outside! Let's get dressed to play in the snow!"

Scarf, coat, boots, cap, mittens. "Ready!" says Suchan.

The snow is already deep.

First, Suchan, Elena, and Goldie play.

Next, they run and spin and fall on their backs. They wave their arms and legs to make snow angels.

chilly: cold

Plot: Sequence
What is the first thing Suchan does in the snow? What does he do after that?

Suchan looks up at the sky. "Snow does dance!"

Then, Dad comes outside. Suchan opens his mouth wide and catches snowflakes on his tongue. "Snow is icy!" he says. Just like his father had told him.

Last, Mom comes outside with a carrot and a hat. They all build a snowman together.

"Snow is for building!" says Suchan.

Dad brings out a sled. Suchan slides down the hill. "Whee!" he says. He has never had so much fun.

Suchan jumps up with excitement. "Snow dances and flies like a fairy. It's cold and made of ice. It slips and slides. And it is good for building. *Now* I know what snow is!"

Visualize

How do you visualize Suchan at the end of the story? Can you show the expression on his face? What details in the text help you to visualize this?

Genre

Realistic Fiction:
Realistic fiction has characters that act like real people.

grumbling: complain

Plot: Sequence

Think Aloud

When we read, it helps to pay attention to the sequence, or what happens first, next, and last. Let's look for the first event to happen in this story. I think that the first thing to happen is that it starts to storm. This is important because the children can't go to the zoo. Now, let's pay attention to what happens next.

Storm Music

Outside, it is raining. Inside, Sara, Daniel, and Sofia are **grumbling**.

"Why does it have to rain on a Saturday?" asks Sara.

"Tia Val was going to take us to the zoo!" says Daniel.

"Maybe it will stop soon," says Sofia.

Crash! Boom!

"Thunder!" says Sara.

Daniel and Sofia cover their ears. "We'll never get to see the elephants!" says Daniel.

"It's not fair," they all say together. "It can't rain on a Saturday!"

Tia Val walks into the room.

"Why does it have to rain?" asks Sara.

"Rain is important," says Tia Val. "Plants and animals and people all need the water that rain brings us."

"But why did it have to rain today?" asks Daniel.

"Rain just happens," says Tia Val "That's how weather works."

"Will it rain all day?" asks Sofia.

"This rainstorm will pass by quickly." Tia Val smiles. "Be **patient**. In the meantime, we can make storm music!"

"What's that?" asked the kids.

"We'll pretend we're the storm," says Tia Val, "and make storm sounds with our bodies."

Sara giggles at that.

Everyone sits on the living room floor. "I'll make a sound with my body," says Tia Val. Watch and *listen*. "When it's your turn, you copy me. Sara, you join in first, then Daniel and then Sofia."

"The sounds will get louder with more people!" says Daniel.

"Yes, yes!" says Sara. "The way a real storm sounds as it gets bigger."

Tia Val rubs her hands together quickly. "First, comes *viento*, the wind." Whish-whish-whish.

Sara rubs her hands together. Whish-whish-whish.

Realistic Fiction
How are the children acting like real children? How is Tia Val acting like a real aunt?

patient: waiting for something without getting upset

Daniel rubs his hands together. Whish-whish-whish

Sofia rubs her hands together. Whish-whish-whish

WHISH-WHISH-WHISH

"Next come *gotas de illuvia*, raindrops," says Tia Val. She taps one finger against her other hand. Tap-tap-tap

Sara taps her finger. Tap-tap-tap

Daniel taps his finger. Tap-tap-tap

Sofia taps her finger. Tap-tap-tap

TAP-TAP-TAP

"Now it rains harder, *torrencialmente*!" Tia Val says. She slaps her knees loudly. Slap-slap-slap.

Sara slaps her knees. Slap-slap-slap.

Daniel slaps his knees. Slap-slap-slap

Sofia slaps her knees. Slap-slap-slap

SLAP-SLAP-SLAP

"Last comes *el trueno*, the thunder!" says Tia Val. She jumps up and **stomps** her feet. Boom-boom-boom

Sara jumps up and stomps her feet. Boom-boom-boom

Daniel jumps up and stomps his feet. Boom-boom-boom

Sofia jumps up and stomps her feet. Boom-boom-boom

BOOM-BOOM-BOOM!

"Look!" says Daniel. "The storm is **passing**. Let's keep moving!"

Boom-boom-boom

Slap-slap-slap

Tap-tap-tap.

Swish-swish-swish . . .

It gets very **calm**.

Drip . . . drip . . . drip. The only sounds are a few drops falling from the roof of the house.

Sara looks outside. "The rain has stopped!"

Everyone runs to the window. Sunshine is breaking through the clouds. Blue sky opens up and a rainbow appears, stretching its colors from one end to the other.

Tia Val smiles. "Now, that's a special surprise."

"I hope all the zoo animals can see it, too," says Daniel.

"We can ask them when we see them," says Tia Val.

"Hurray!" say Sara, Daniel, and Sofia. "Let's go!"

passing: going away

Visualize
The sounds words are getting quieter. How do you think the children are moving now?

calm: quiet

Plot: Sequence
What is the last thing to happen in this story?

Ms. Squeakers

Becky wanted a dog. But her parents got her a guinea pig instead.

"I had a guinea pig when I was little," said her dad. "Mr. Oinky was the best pet I ever had."

"But a guinea pig won't jump up to **greet** me when I come home from school," said Becky.

"Mr. Oinky sat on my desk and helped me do homework," said her dad. "That was very helpful."

They brought the guinea pig home from the pet shop and put the cage in Becky's room. Becky got down on her knees and looked at her new pet.

"Hello," she said. The guinea pig looked back. It wiggled its nose, but didn't say anything. Then it lay down and took a nap.

Becky really wished her parents had gotten her a dog and not a guinea pig.

She took out a copy of her favorite book, *Dog Heroes*. She read the part where a dalmation barks to **inform** its owner of danger. A dalmation would be the perfect pet.

At dinner that night, Becky asked, "When can I get a dog?"

"You just got a guinea pig!" said her mom.

"But a guinea pig won't bark to warn me of danger," said Becky

"Have you been reading again?" asked her mom.

"Mr. Oinky was black and white, just like your guinea pig, and just like a dalmation!" said her dad. "Have you thought of a name yet?"

"Not yet," said Becky. "I'm waiting for him to do something interesting." But Becky couldn't imagine what kind of interesting thing a guinea pig could do.

Later, Becky said good night to the guinea pig. But the guinea pig was already asleep, curled up at the back of its cage.

inform: tell someone a fact

Make, Confirm, and Revise Predictions

Think Aloud

Remember, we can make predictions about what we think will happen in a text. Here I read that Becky is asking when she can get a dog. I predict her parents will surprise her with a dog. Let's listen to see if my prediction is correct.

squeeaakk

ignore: does not pay attention to

replied: answered

underestimated: did not realize how good something was

"Oh, I wish I had a dog," thought Becky. "A dog would sleep at the bottom of my bed."

The next day Becky was building a castle in her room when she heard a very loud *squeeeaaaakkkk*. It was the guinea pig. Becky tried her best to **ignore** the sound. She put on another block and then she heard it again. *Squeeak!!!*

Becky looked up and could see part of her castle tipping over. She quickly propped up the falling pieces.

"Thanks for the warning," she said to the guinea pig. It **replied** with a small squeak.

Becky watched her new pet for a while. Then she said, "Maybe I **underestimated** you."

After that, Becky began to pay more attention to the guinea pig. She took it out of its cage as soon as she got home from school, and noticed that it always had its nose pressed up against the glass when she came in.

She also realized that the guinea pig was a very good listener. Becky would tell it all about her day, and it wiggled its nose at all the right parts. The more time Becky spent with the guinea pig, the more she found they had in common!

Her mom wouldn't let the guinea pig sleep in her bed, but it napped in Becky's lap when she did her homework. Its favorite subject was math, just like hers! They both always enjoyed a crunchy snack of cucumber slices. And they loved watching the world go by together, out their bedroom window.

One day, Becky's dad stopped into her room and asked, "So do you still want a dog?"

"No," said Becky. "I think Ms. Squeakers is the best pet I'll ever have."

Make, Confirm, and Revise Predictions
Do you still think Becky will get a dog as we predicted? Why or why not? Do you have a new prediction?

Plot: Problem and Solution
What was Becky's problem in the beginning? How did she solve her problem?

Genre

Realistic Fiction: Characters in realistic fiction can have feelings like real people.

Character, Setting, Plot

Think Aloud

When we read, it helps to think about the character and the plot. This story is about a girl named Isabella. She is the character. She seems very proud of all the things she can do. Now she wants to learn how to ride a bike. That will be the plot. Let's pay attention to what Isabella does to learn to ride a bike.

accomplish: do something difficult

My First Bike Ride

My name is Isabella Abigail Garcia. I'm six years old and four feet tall.

I can run and climb to the tippy-top of the jungle gym.

I can build a whole castle out of blocks, tie my own shoes, and count to one hundred!

But I can't ride a bike.

Yet.

I've been practicing every day after school.

Mom says that I can **accomplish** anything if I practice enough.

Today, I climb onto my bike and pedal very fast.

"Look at me!" I yell. "I'm really riding!"

Then I fall to one side. I'm glad the grass is soft.

I climb back onto my bike and pedal very slow.

"You can do it!" I say to myself. I bite down on my lips.

I fall to the other side. I'm glad I'm wearing a helmet.

I climb onto my bike and lean forward while I ride.

I fall again. Now I am used to it.

I climb onto my bike and lean back when I ride.

I fall to the other side.

I give my bike a talking to.

"You better behave yourself," I say.

But my bike doesn't look like it's listening.

Make, Confirm, and Revise Predictions

Think Aloud

When we read, it helps to make predictions about what we think will happen. I see that Isabella keeps falling off her bike. And now she says her bike isn't listening to her. I predict that she will not try to ride anymore today. Maybe she will go and do another activity. And then she will learn how to ride a bike later.

triumphant:
successful

confidence: belief
that you can do it

Realistic Fiction

*Characters in realistic
fiction can have
feelings like real
people. How is Isabella
feeling when she talks
to Mom?*

**Make, Confirm,
Revise Predictions**

*Was my prediction
about Isabella not
riding more today
correct? How can we
revise it? What do
you think will happen
now?*

I think it's time for a snack.

Inside, I tell Mom that riding a bike is harder than it looks. I eat apple slices and cry a little bit, too.

Mom gives me a hug. She says that I am brave.

I want to be brave.

She says that she knows I will learn to ride if I keep trying. She says I've almost got it. Mom is usually right. I hope she is right this time too.

I eat the rest of my apple slices very slowly, but soon they are all gone.

Mom says she'll be watching. She says she knows I will return **triumphant**.

I walk back outside. I climb back on my bike, but I don't start pedaling yet. I wave at Mom.

"Just have **confidence** in yourself!" she calls.

I take a deep breath.

This time I don't pedal too fast and I don't pedal too slow.

I don't lean forward and I don't lean back. I don't look at my bike. I look at the tree across the yard. And I **concentrate**.

The tree is getting closer! I'm not falling over!

Mom was right.

My name is Isabella Abigail Garcia. I'm six year old and four feet (and now one inch extra) tall.

I can kick a soccer ball a long way and blow bubbles under water. I can spell the word alligator (a-l-l-i-g-a-t-o-r), give my little sister a piggy-back ride, and RIDE A BIKE!

But I can't ride a **unicycle**.

Yet.

concentrate: pay close attention

unicycle: a bike with one wheel

Character, Setting, Plot

What happens at the end of the story? Why does Isabella end the story with the word, "Yet." What does this tell you about her?

Genre

Realistic Fiction:
Realistic fiction often
has a message or a
lesson.

Mia's Turn

It was almost time for school. Mia ran into the kitchen where Grandpa was finishing up today's surprise.

"Close your eyes!" Grandpa announced. "Today's lunch is . . .,"

Mia couldn't help herself. She peeked. "Pinwheel sandwiches!" she squealed.

She loved Grandpa's lunches almost as much as she loved Grandpa. He finished slicing the rolled tortillas and put six circle sandwiches in Mia's lunch. She chose a banana, Grandpa added carrots, and Mom looked at her watch. "Time to go," she said.

Grandpa wrapped Mia in a hug. "I won't do a thing until you get back."

"Silly Grandpa," Mia said, hugging back.

Ask and Answer Questions

Think Aloud

As we read, it helps to ask questions about things we don't understand. Then we can try to answer the questions. I read that Grandpa tells Mia he won't do a thing until she gets back. I ask myself how that can be. Then I read on and see that Mia says, "Silly Grandpa." That means Grandpa was joking. Now I understand.

When school got out, Mom was still working, so Grandpa picked Mia up. On the walk home, Mia told Grandpa about her day and he told her about his.

In the afternoons they played games. Today, Grandpa pulled a box from behind his back. "Puzzles," he said.

"Those are easy," Mia said.

"This puzzle has 48 pieces." Grandpa dumped the pieces onto the table.

"That's more than we've ever done," Mia said. She wondered if she'd be able finish.

"One piece at a time," Grandpa said, **reassuring** her.

While Grandpa sorted the colors, Mia stood the box on its side, so they could see what they were making.

"Hmm," said Grandpa. "Let's start with corners and edges."

"Here's an edge," said Mia. "And a corner!"

Before long, the puzzle was finished. "I **suspected** we could figure it out," Grandpa said.

Ask and Answer Questions
What questions do you have about Grandpa and Mia?

reassuring: making feel better

suspected: believed

Plot: Sequence

Think Aloud

When we read, it helps to pay attention to the order in which things happen. This means to think about what happens first, next, *and* last. *Today Grandpa has to stay in bed. Mia knows just how to help. I see that the first thing she does is make Grandpa food that she decorated in a fun way just as Grandpa decorates her lunches. Let's pay attention to what she does next to help Grandpa.*

In the evenings, Grandpa would read to Mia from her favorite books. Sometimes the stories were about silly things, like elephants driving cars. Other times they were about real things, like gorillas living in the jungle. Grandpa's stories were the best part of Mia's day. After the last was read, Grandpa would sing the songs his mother had sung to him. Before long, Mia would fall asleep. In the morning, she'd wake to another lunch surprise, more games, and more stories.

One Saturday morning everything changed.

"Grandpa hurt his foot," Mom said. "He has to stay in bed for a few weeks."

Mia thought of all of the best things Grandpa did for her. She knew just how to help.

First, while Mom heated water for minty tea, Mia made breakfast. She spread a layer of peanut butter over a waffle and made a silly face with raisins and bananas.

"What's this?" Grandpa asked when Mia and Mom entered with a tray of breakfast goodies.

"Peanut butter banana surprise," Mia said.

"Yum!" said Grandpa. "Have you been taking cooking lessons?"

Mia giggled. "Silly Grandpa."

Later that morning, Mia tapped on Grandpa's door **cautiously**. She didn't want to wake him up.

"Is it time for games?" he asked.

"Close your eyes," she said and pulled something from behind her back.

"A puzzle!" Grandpa said.

"Not just any puzzle," Mia said. "This one has 60 pieces."

"Are we ready for such a **challenge**?" Grandpa asked.

"One piece at a time," Mia said reassuringly.

In the evening, just before bed, Grandpa asked Mia to read from her favorite books. She didn't know all of the words, but that didn't matter. She knew the stories **by heart**.

By the time the last story had been read, Grandpa was feeling better, so Mia sang the songs he'd sung to her so many times. Before long, Grandpa was snoring. Mia tiptoed out of the room singing her Grandpa's favorite lullaby.

cautiously: to do carefully in case something bad happens

challenge: something difficult

by heart: to know from memory

Realistic Fiction
What lessons do you think Mia learned from Grandpa? How is she showing it?

Plot: Sequence
What is the last thing Mia does to help make Grandpa feel better?

shrugged: raised shoulders; often means "I don't know"

nervous: worried

Plot: Cause and Effect

Think Aloud

If we have a question about a story event, it helps to think about what caused it to happen. That means to understand why something happens.

I wondered why Cameron was the only kid who doesn't cheer because there are three days of school left. When I read on, I see that he was nervous about being a first grader. That is why he didn't cheer.

Cameron Loves Kindergarten

Mr. Holmes drew a big black X over another white square on the calendar. There were only a few more white squares left before the yellow star. And Cameron knew just what the star meant. The last day of school.

"Only 3 more days of school! And then you'll be first graders!" Mr. Holmes said.

The kids sitting around Cameron cheered. Everyone but Cameron.

"Aren't you excited about summer vacation?" asked Jack, who was sitting next to him.

Cameron **shrugged**. He was excited for vacation. But he wasn't excited about being a first grader. He got more and more **nervous** each day as the white boxes were filled in with Xs.

Kindergarten was great. He liked his teacher, Mr. Holmes. He liked the drawings that covered the walls (some of them by Cameron!), and he liked the other kids, especially his best friends, Jack and Abby. But more than anything else, Cameron liked Morton, the class lizard.

Way back in September, Cameron hadn't known all the things he liked about kindergarten. Sometimes he felt sad when his dad dropped him off at school. But then Mr. Holmes gave Cameron a very special job; feeding Morton his breakfast. Once a week, he even got to feed Morton a banana. After that Cameron didn't mind being dropped off at school. And he even figured out all the other things he liked about kindergarten too.

"Today we're making a special visit to the first grade so you can meet your new teacher and see your new classroom," said Mr. Holmes.

Oh no, thought Cameron! He didn't even want to think about first grade.

But the rest of the class was already lining up. Cameron could see Morton's tiny tongue **flicking** in and out of his mouth across the room. He was already hungry. Poor Morton.

Realistic Fiction
How did Cameron feel about kindergarten in the beginning of the year? How is it similar to the way he feels now?

flicking: moving suddenly and sharply

hesitated: waited

Make, Confirm, and Revise Predictions

(**Think Aloud**)

As we read, it can help to make predictions. about what we think will happen. I know that Cameron is nervous about first grade. Now, Ms. Rylant is talking to him. I think he will be too shy to talk to her. Let's read on to find out if my prediction is correct.

Cameron lined up with Jack and Abby and they all went together down the hall to first grade. Cameron looked around the first grade classroom. It wasn't at all like kindergarten. And none of the drawing on the walls were by Cameron and his friends. Ms. Rylant looked nothing like Mr. Holmes. And of course, there was no Morton.

"Welcome!" said Ms. Rylant. "I'm looking forward to getting to know all of you next year! Please have a look around the classroom."

All the other kids began spinning globes and poking around bookshelves. Cameron **hesitated** by the door.

Ms. Rylant walked over.

"Hello," she said. "Don't you want to look around?"

"No," said Cameron. "I think I'd rather stay in kindergarten."

"Ah," said Ms. Rylant. "Kindergarten is pretty great. Are you Cameron, by chance?"

Cameron nodded. How did she know his name?

"I've heard you're quite the lizard man," Ms. Rylant said. "Come on, I have something to show you."

In the very back corner of the classroom, Ms. Rylant pointed to a low shelf.

"Allow me to **introduce** you. Cameron, meet Humphrey. Humphrey, meet Cameron," she said.

Cameron's eyes widened. Humphrey was a lizard! And not just any lizard, a bearded dragon lizard! And his tongue was flicking in and out.

"He looks hungry," said Cameron.

"Would you like to feed him?" asked Ms. Rylant. "He gets apple for breakfast."

Back in kindergarten, a little later, Cameron told Morton all about Humphrey. "He's bigger than you, but not nearly as green. And guess what he likes for breakfast? Apple! Have you ever tried apple?" said Cameron. "But the very best part is that Ms. Rylant said you could come visit! So you can meet Humphrey yourself! It's a little different from kindergarten, but I think you are really going to like the first grade."

Morton took a giant bite of banana, and Cameron was sure he was excited, too.

Make, Confirm, and Revise Predictions
Was our prediction about Cameron being too shy to talk to Ms. Rylant correct? Now what do you predict will happen when he talks to Ms. Rylant?

introduce: meet someone for the first time

Plot: Cause and Effect
What caused Cameron to change his mind about first grade?

Fantasy

Who are the characters in this story so far? What are they doing?

Key Details

Think Aloud

Remember, we can focus on key details that tell what a story is really about. Here Elrod is worried that he will forget his playdate with Antelope. This is because he often forgets things. I think this is a key detail. Let's read on to find out if he remembers.

appointment: when you are supposed to meet someone

Elrod the Elephant Remembers

Elrod, the little elephant, met Antelope at the watering hole. The two splashed each other all morning long. They had so much fun together that Antelope invited Elrod over to play the next week.

"Next Thursday, on the savannah. Don't forget!" said Antelope, saying goodbye.

Elrod waved his trunk happily, but as soon as Antelope was gone, he began to worry. And he worried all the way back to the acacia grove, where his friends Baboon, Giraffe, and Egret were having lunch. He worried because unlike most elephants, Elrod did often forget things. Last summer, he had forgotten Zebra's going-away party. Just last week, he had forgotten his **appointment** with Plover Bird to have his teeth cleaned. One year he'd even forgotten his own birthday!

remind: a way to remember something

craned: stretched to see something

Baboon noticed Elrod looking sad and asked, "What's the matter, Elrod?"

"I am worried I will forget my play date with Antelope next Thursday on the savannah and then he won't want to be my new friend anymore," Elrod answered.

"Don't worry, Elrod," said Baboon. "You can tie a string around your finger to **remind** yourself! That is what I always do." Baboon held up his hand and spread his long fingers.

"But, Baboon," said Elrod, "I don't have any fingers!" He stomped his round feet just to show Baboon.

"Don't worry, Elrod!" said Giraffe, "You can leave yourself a note on my bulletin branch. That is what I always do."

Elrod **craned** his neck, but it was no use. "Thank you, Giraffe," he said, "but your bulletin branch is much too high for me to see!"

Key Details

Think Aloud

Remember, we can pay attention to key details to understand a story better. Here I read that the friends are trying to help Elrod by sharing how they remember things. Baboon ties a string around his finger. But Elrod doesn't have a finger. These are key details. Next, giraffe has a bulletin board but Elrod can't see it. These are key details too. Let's pay attention to more key details as we read.

chatter: little sounds; talk that doesn't meaning anything

bellowed: yelled

raspy: voice that sounds tired and weak

Key Details

How does Egret remember things? Why can't Elrod use Egret's way of remembering things?

"Don't worry, Elrod," said Egret. "When I want to remember something, I always **chatter** it to myself over and over, like this: *Rick-rack, rick-rack, rick-rack!* Why don't you try?"

Elrod **bellowed**, "Next Thursday on the savannah," over and over, but after only a minute his throat felt dry and his voice was **raspy.**

"It's no use," he said. "My voice is not made to chatter like yours, Egret."

He hung his head. "I will never remember my play date with Antelope, and she will not want to be my new friend anymore."

"But you are my old friend, Elrod," said Baboon. "So I will tie a string around my finger to remember your play date and I will remind you."

"Yes, you are my old friend, too, Elrod," said Giraffe. "So I will post a note about your play date on my bulletin branch and I will also remind you."

"And don't forget me!" said Egret. "I am your oldest friend, so I will chatter to myself about your play date all week and I too will remind you!"

Elrod was overjoyed. With three such wise old friends to remind him, he would never forget his play date with Antelope. And then he had his own idea.

"If you three are going to remember my play date for me," he said, "then you three should also come to my play date with me! Antelope will surely be happy to have four new friends instead of one!"

And she surely was.

Ask and Answer Questions
How does Elrod remember the playdate? What else does he do? What questions do you have about the ending of this story?

Plot: Sequence

Tiny and the Windy Day

One spring day, Tiny the Spider was out walking when suddenly the wind began to blow.

Whish, Whoosh, Whish went the wind.

The grass **swayed** back and forth. The leaves blew this way and that.

Even the tree branches bent down to the ground.

"Oh my!" said Tiny the Spider. "A windy day is the WORST kind of day for a tiny spider like me!"

Tiny grabbed the nearest wildflower and held on tight. But the wind was too strong and she fell to the ground. Then she started to run. She went as fast as her eight little legs could carry her, trying to **avoid** the wind. But the wind kept on blowing.

Whish, Whoosh, Whish went the wind.

2

Tiny passed a caterpillar. "Oh, Caterpillar!" she cried. "Please help me. I am Tiny the Spider. A windy day is the WORST kind of day for a **delicate** thing like me. What can I do so that I won't blow away?"

"You are certainly very tiny," said the caterpillar. "And I would hate for you to get blown away. Here is an idea. Lie down in the grass and pull in your legs. That way the wind won't be able to reach you."

So Tiny lay down in the grass and pulled in her legs. She became like a tiny ball. She waited and worried and waited and worried and then she heard it.

Whish, Whoosh, Whish went the wind.

The tree branches swayed, the leaves blew, and the wind reached deep into the grass where Tiny lay. The wind kept blowing and Tiny began to roll like a ball! It felt like the wind was chasing her.

Whish, Whoosh, Whish went the wind.

"Help!" cried Tiny. "I am rolling like a ball."

Tiny rolled and rolled until she hit something. She opened her eyes and saw a tree.

delicate: something that is small and breaks easily

Visualize

(Think Aloud)

As we read, it helps to visualize what the text is saying. This means to make a picture in your mind. Here, the text says that Tiny lay down and pulled her legs in so that she became like a ball. I can picture that. She is pretty round. Her legs look like they can fold in. This helps me to understand how she starts rolling so fast.

3

"Oh, tree!" cried Tiny. "Thank goodness you are here. A windy day is the WORST kind of day for a tiny spider like me. I will stay close to you so I don't blow away!"

Tiny **huddled** against the tree. She waited and worried and waited and worried.

Whish, Whoosh, Whish went the wind.

And the wind came and lifted Tiny up into the air.

"Oh, no!" she cried. The wind blew harder and threw Tiny high up into the sky. Then she fell and landed on the tree.

"Oh, dear!" cried Tiny. She had never been so high up before! How would she ever get down?

She remembered that she had once seen her mother float through the sky on a balloon made of her own silk. Maybe she could do it, too!

First, she stood on tiptoes. Next, she began to shoot silk into the air just like she had seen her mother do.

Whish, Whoosh, Whish went the wind.

The wind caught the silk and Tiny floated up.

huddled: leaned into

Plot: Sequence

What is the first thing that Tiny does to help her float through the sky? What does she do next?

60   Fantasy

Up, up, up she went. All the way to the sky.

Soon she was dancing in the wind.

"Whee!" she said and started to laugh.

"Hello!" came a voice. "It took you long enough to get here."

Tiny turned around in surprise. She saw another tiny spider floating in the wind just as she was. This spider was **dangling** from its own silk and swaying back and forth.

"Hello!" said Tiny. "I didn't know we could fly."

Then she heard more giggles. She looked around. Dozens of tiny spiders were dancing in the wind.

"Isn't it fun!" said the first little spider.

Whish, Whoosh, Whish went the wind.

"Yes," said Tiny with **delight**. "Now I know that a windy day is the BEST kind of day for a tiny spider like me!"

Visualize

Visualize Tiny as she sees the first little spider. How is she moving? What does the expression on her face look like?

dangling: swinging

delight: happiness and joy

Plot: Cause and Effect

Think Aloud

As we read, let's think about the reasons why things happen. We call that "cause and effect." A cause is the reason something happens. The effect is what happens. I read that Clyde is tired of the same burrow. That is what causes him to go out and look for a better home.

burrow: a hole where animals live

clambered: climbed with effort

basking: soaking up warmth and good feelings

A Home for Clyde

Most days, Clyde was happy in the woody brush he called home. Just like all the other armidillos. But today was different. He was tired of the same **burrow**, in the same dusty scrubland where he'd lived since he was a pink pup. Maybe he could find a better home. He sniffed the air and moved his head from side to side. Which way should he go?

As Clyde's brothers **clambered** out of the burrow, heading one way, Clyde went another; beyond the scrub, down a sandy bank to the edge of the river, where he met TURTLE.

"Hello, Turtle!" Clyde called. "What are you doing?"

Turtle stretched his long neck and opened a lazy eye.

"**Basking** in the sun," he said. "You're welcome to join me."

Clyde studied the rock where Turtle had been dozing. It looked bumpy and hard to climb. Turtle's claws were just right for rocks. Clyde's were just right for digging.

"Thanks for the offer," Clyde said, "but your claws are small. Mine are big. Too big for climbing slippery rocks. I'll be on my way."

"Good day," said Turtle.

Clyde sniffed the air, swung his head side to side, and moved along. Soon, he heard MOCKINGBIRD whistling a song.

"Hello, Mockingbird!" Clyde called. "What are you doing?"

Mockingbird ruffled her feathers. "I'm singing, of course. Would you care to join me?"

Mockingbird was sitting on the tallest branch of a mesquite tree.

"Your home is high and I can't fly," Clyde said.

"Can you try?" asked Mockingbird.

Clyde stood on his two back legs. His scaly shell was heavy. His **stubby** arms were not the same as wings. He could never fly to a home high in the branches.

Plot: Cause and Effect
What does Clyde do when Turtle invites him onto his rock? Why does he do that?

Fantasy
What parts of this story could not happen in real life?

stubby: short and thick

reputation: what many people think about somone or something.

Make, Confirm, and Revise Predictions

Think Aloud

As we read it helps to make predictions about what we think will happen. I know that Turtle's home and Mockingbird's home were not right for Clyde. But a badger lives in a burrow just like an armadillo. I predict Clyde will like this home. As we read on, let's check to see if this prediction is correct.

"I tried," said Clyde. "But your tree is not for me. I'll be on my way."

"Perhaps another day," said Mockingbird.

Before long, Clyde reached a spot with short brown grass and open space. He came to a burrow that reminded him of the one he'd left behind.

Clyde called, "Anybody home?"

"Go away," came a voice from deep inside.

"BADGER, is that you?" Clyde asked.

But, Badger didn't say a word.

Clyde tried again. "What's new?"

Still no answer.

Badger had a **reputation** for grumpiness. Clyde put his head in and Badger growled.

"Oh, no," thought Clyde. "Badger's home will never do. Badger's home is not for two."

"Till next time," Clyde said. And off he went.

Clyde was getting tired. His home could not be a rock or a tree. He did not want to share a burrow with someone grumpy.

At last, he came to a sunny shore. He scuttled into the water and sank to the bottom. There, he came face to face with two big eyes.

"Hello, BASS!" said Clyde. "What's new?"

"Not much," said Bass, "How about you?"

"Passing through," said Clyde. He liked crossing the pond, but he couldn't stay underwater forever. A pond would never be home for an armadillo.

He waved goodbye and made his way to the other side, up and out of the water. There, on the shore, were his three brothers!

"Hello, Clyde," said the middle brother.

"Where have you been?" asked the oldest.

"Glad you're home," said the youngest.

"Home," said Clyde. After visiting his friends, this was exactly where he wanted to be.

"Home," he said again.

Most days, Clyde was happy living in the woody brush. Today, he was happier than ever.

Make, Confirm, and Revise Predictions

Does Clyde stay with Badger as we predicted? What do you predict he will do about finding a new home?

Genre

Fantasy: Fantasy stories can have fantasy characters in realistic settings.

Fantasy

What parts of this story tell about what really happens in spring? What parts are fantasy?

tramped: walked heavily

dotted: lightly covered with little patches

Spring Is Here!

Benjamin Bear woke from a long winter's nap. He peeked out the window. The sun was rising. He opened the door. The air felt warmer. He sniffed. "Spring is coming!" he said. "I must tell Groundhog."

Benjamin **tramped** over the last patches of snow. The trees were bare except for tight green buds that **dotted** the branches. He reached Groundhog's hole and knocked on the door.

"Who's there?" Groundhog called from deep inside his burrow.

"It's me, Benjamin Bear!" He peeked in. The house was dark.

Benjamin Bear switched on the lights and stood beside Groundhog, who was resting on the couch.

"Good morning, Groundhog. Spring is coming."

"Impossible," said Groundhog. He rolled over and **groaned**. "Is the ground still white with snow?"

"It's melting. Soon the grass will grow," said Benjamin.

"Please, can you come back later?" asked Groundhog.

Benjamin sighed. "I'll wake the others and be back soon."

He turned off the lights and went to find Chipmunk.

On the way, Benjamin spied a purple flower peeking out of the dirt. When he arrived at Chipmunk's door, there was a sign that said, "Do Not **Disturb**!" Benjamin knew Chipmunk loved flowers. Wouldn't she want to hear the good news? Spring was near! He knocked and before long, Chipmunk appeared at the window.

"Is that you, Benjamin?"

"Spring is coming. I saw a purple flower!" said Benjamin.

Chipmunk opened the door and invited Benjamin inside.

groaned: make a deep unhappy noise

disturb: bother

Plot: Sequence

Think Aloud

We can think about sequence, or the order in which things happen, to help us understand a story better. Benjamin is visiting different animals to tell them about spring. I know the first animal he visited was Groundhog. Who is the next animal he visits? That's right, it's Chipmunk. Let's look for who Benjamin tells about spring next.

Think Aloud

Here the text says, small green sprouts (are) poking out of the soil. *I try to visualize, or make a picture in my mind, of these words. I can see plants when they are first growing. A tiny bit of green is coming out of the dark soil. I also picture the last patches of snow.*

Visualize

Close your eyes and visualize these words, Soon the clouds gathered in the sky and it began to drizzle. *What are you imagining?*

patches: small pieces of something

drizzle: light rain

"Spring will be here sooner than you think," said Benjamin.

"I think," said Chipmunk, "it would be nice to sleep a few days longer." She yawned and stretched and curled into a tiny ball of fur.

Benjamin tiptoed away. "I'll wake the others and be back soon," he whispered.

By now, the sun was higher in the sky. The last **patches** of snow were melting and the ground was warming. Benjamin noticed small green sprouts poking, here and there, out of the soil.

"Spring is coming!" said Benjamin.

"Shh . ." said Ground Squirrel. "I'm trying to sleep."

Soon, clouds gathered in the sky and it began to **drizzle**. Up from the mud came Frog.

"Spring is coming," said Benjamin.

Frog began to peep and sing, "Spring is coming! Spring is coming!" Soon his frog friends joined the loud **chorus**.

chorus: a group singing

Benjamin Bear sat by the pond and listened to the first songs of spring. Before long, the geese arrived, honking a welcoming song. Soon after, the queen bee awoke, and the bees started humming a buzzing song. The birds chirped and the sun returned to brighten the sky.

"Time to wake our friends," said Benjamin.

The bees and birds, geese and frogs joined in. They sang loud and LOUDER and soon, out of their homes came Ground Squirrel and Chipmunk and, even, Groundhog. It seemed to Benjamin that the whole world was singing

"Spring is here," said all of the animals.

"I knew it!" said Benjamin Bear. "Spring is HERE!"

Plot: Sequence
What is the last thing to happen in this story?

A Rainbow for Snail

All day it rained and poured. All day the animals stayed **tucked** inside their houses.

At last, the rain stopped and Mole peeked out of her hole. She looked at the sky. She saw red and yellow and orange. She saw green and blue and violet.

"Listen, everyone!" she called. "Come to my hill as quick as you can to see the rainbow."

Mole did this whenever a rainbow appeared. And all of the animals knew just what to do.

Bird flew as fast as she could to Mole's hill. "Spectacular!" she said when she saw the rainbow.

Butterfly fluttered all the way to Mole's hill. "Remarkable!" he said when he saw the rainbow.

Grasshopper hopped to the top of Mole's hill. "Magnificent," she cried when she saw the rainbow.

The animals **gathered** on Mole's hill and looked at the sky. They oohed and aahed over the rainbow, just like always.

All but Snail. Snail had never seen the rainbow before. He was just too slow to climb up Mole's hill. And there was nothing that he wanted more than to see all of the colors, all together, just like he had heard about.

This time when he heard Mole's call, he was ready. He puts his head down just as he always did when he wanted to go fast.

He chugged and he slugged. He inched and he pinched. He slid and he pushed his way up the hill. Slowly, slowly, slowly.

"Hurry up, Snail!" called the other animals. "You will miss the rainbow again!"

"Oh, no," thought Snail. He lowered his head even more, just like he always did when he wanted to go fast. He closed his eyes to **concentrate**.

He chugged and he slugged. He inched and he pinched. He slid and he pushed his way up the hill.

"Where is the rainbow?" he asked when he arrived. He huffed and puffed in exhaustion.

Plot: Problem and Solution

Think Aloud

When we read a story, it can help to think about the problem a character needs to solve. Here I read that Snail can never get to Mole's hill to see the rainbow. That is a problem. As we read, let's look for ways that Snail tries to solve his problem.

concentrate: pay attention to what you are doing

3

disappeared: cannot be seen anymore

disappointed: sad that something didn't happen

Make, Confirm, and Revise Predictions

Think Aloud

Remember that good readers make predictions about what will happen in a story. Here Snail says he will see the rainbow for sure because he will go as fast as he can. I think he won't see the rainbow. He is already going as fast as he can. Let's read on to see if my prediction is correct.

"Snail!" said the other animals. "You are too late again! The rainbow has **disappeared**. Can't you get here any faster?"

Snail was **disappointed** once again. "Next time, I will be fast enough to see the rainbow," he said.

Weeks passed. At last, it rained again. When the rain stopped, Snail listened to see if there was a rainbow.

"Listen, everyone!" called Mole. "Come to my hill as fast as you can to see the rainbow!"

Once again, Snail put his head down as he always did when he wanted to go fast. He chugged and he slugged. He inched and he pinched. He slid and he pulled his way up the hill. But once again he was too late.

"Next time I will see the rainbow for sure," he told himself. "I will go as fast as I possibly can!"

It rained a few weeks later. And as soon as Snail heard Mole's call, he set out. He put his head down just as he always did when he wanted to go fast. He shut his eyes to help him concentrate. He slugged and he chugged. He inched and he pinched. He bumped into something hard. He lifted his head and opened his eyes and saw Turtle.

"Snail! Why are you rushing with your eyes closed like that?" asked Turtle.

"I don't have time to talk, Turtle," said Snail. "I have to hurry to Mole's house to see the rainbow."

"It is a particularly beautiful rainbow," said Turtle.

"How did you get to Mole's house and back so quickly!?" asked Snail.

Turtle lifted her head and looked up at the sky.

"The rainbow isn't just at Mole's house," said Turtle. "All you have to do is look up at the sky."

Snail lifted his head and looked up at the sky.

And there it was. Red, orange, and yellow. Green, blue, and purple. A rainbow! It was the best thing Snail had ever seen. And all he had to do to see it was look in the sky.

Make, Confirm, and Revise Predictions
I predicted that Snail would not see the rainbow. But now Turtle says she has already seen the rainbow. How can we revise my prediction?

Plot: Problem and Solution
What was Snail's problem? How did he solve it?

Fantasy

Are these animals like real animals? Why or why not?

accidentally: by mistake

Reread

Think Aloud

Little Bear is telling Big Bear it's too early in the morning to sing. I wonder why he is saying that. To help me understand, I can go back and reread the parts that came before. It says, "All of the other animals are still sleeping." That explains it. Little Bear is worried Big Bear is making too much noise and will wake the other animals.

Big Bear Thinks of Others

One morning, Big Bear and Little Bear wake up early.

"Let's watch the sun rise," says Big Bear.

Little Bear loves the colors at sunrise. "Yes! Let's go!"

The two friends leave their den and walk through the forest. Big Bear leads the way while Little Bear hurries to keep up.

Squash! Little Bear looks up. Big Bear **accidentally** steps right on Rabbit's burrow door. But he keeps on walking. Little Bear hurries to keep up. But he worries about Rabbit's burrow.

All of the animals are still sleeping. Big Bear says, "I love singing in the morning!" He sings loudly, *"Good morning to you! Good morning to you!"*

"Shh," says Little Bear. "It's too early in the morning."

2

Suddenly, Little Bear hears crying.

Big Bear's singing woke up Mrs. Fox's babies. Little Bear scurries to keep up with Big Bear but worries when he sees Mrs. Fox **fussing** over her unhappy babies.

When Little Bear catches up, Big Bear is sitting in the middle of a blueberry bush, popping the last berry into his mouth. "Mmm-mmm. Yum!"

Little Bear stops. His stomach growls. All that hurrying and scurrying has made him hungry. He is upset. He would have liked some berries, too.

"Big Bear!" he says. "You stepped on Rabbit's burrow. You woke Mrs. Fox's babies. And now you've eaten all the berries. You can't just think about yourself and what you want. You should think about others and how they feel. You have to be **considerate**."

Right then, the first burst of sunlight peeks over the mountain.

Big Bear and Little Bear sit silently, watching the sun come up.

fussing: taking trouble to care for

considerate: thinks about others and how they feel

Plot: Cause and Effect

Think Aloud

When we come to a new story event, it helps to think about what caused that event to happen. Here Little Bear gets upset with Big Bear. I will think about why. I know that Big Bear just ate all of the berries. He also stepped on Rabbit's burrow and woke the fox babies. These are all good reasons, or causes, for Little Bear to be upset.

3

The warm colors calm Little Bear, but Big Bear thinks and thinks. He thinks about Little Bear's words. He didn't mean to hurt anyone or their feelings. He wants to get along with the other animals. He wants everyone to be happy.

When the sun is up, Little Bear says, "I'm sorry I was **cross** with you."

Big Bear smiles at his friend. "You weren't cross, you were trying to help."

As they start home, Big Bear finds another bush full of **plump**, sweet blueberries. "Eat as many as you want," he says.

And Little Bear does.

Then Big Bear goes to Mrs. Fox's den. "Let me help put your babies back to sleep," he says. And he sings a sweet lullaby.

By the time Little Bear catches up, the babies are sleeping and Big Bear is already on his way to Rabbit's burrow, where Rabbit is busy rebuilding his door.

cross: angry

plump: round and full

Reread

Why does Big Bear help Mrs. Fox put her babies to sleep? What part of the text could we reread to tell us?

"I'm sorry I squashed your burrow," says Big Bear. And he helps Rabbit fix his home.

By the time Little Bear catches up, Rabbit is back inside his burrow and Big Bear is almost back at the den.

Inside, Big Bear surprises Little Bear with a special breakfast. Big Bear places peppermint tea and biscuits with honey before Little Bear.

"For me?" asks Little Bear.

"Yes. To thank you for being a considerate friend."

And he gives Little Bear a warm bear hug!

Plot: Cause and Effect

What causes Big Bear to make a special breakfast for Little Bear?

Text Structure: Sequence

Think Aloud

When we read a story it helps to think about sequence, or the order in which events happen. I ask myself what is the first thing to happen in this story. In the beginning the animals all talk about being hungry. I think that is the first event. Let's look for the next event as we continue to read.

spied: saw

The Apple Ladder

Summer was over. The trees and bushes were bare. There was hardly a nut or berry in sight. The animals gathered wondering what to do.

"I'm hungry!" said Rabbit.

"My stomach is growling," said Skunk.

"I've got the smallest stomach of all and it's growling the loudest," said Field Mouse.

Deer looked at the lower branches of the apple tree where the friends had been playing.

No apples.

But when he stepped further back, he **spied** red in the upper branches. "Apples!" he cried. He walked around the tree. "The treetop is full of them!"

"Rabbit," said Field Mouse. "You're the best jumper. Can you jump high enough to reach the apples?"

Rabbit **hop-hop-hopped!**

But he never came close to the apples.

"What if I stand on Deer's back?" asked Skunk.

She climbed onto Deer's back and **s-t-r-e-t-c-h-e-d** as high as she could.

But she never came close to the apples.

"What if we knock them down?" asked Deer.

Skunk and Field Mouse threw rocks, acorns, and pinecones at the apples.

But they never came close to the apples.

It was almost as if those red ripe apples were **teasing** the friends, daring them to come up and pick them.

But how?

teasing: playfully making fun of

Make, Confirm, and Revise Predictions

Think Aloud

Remember, we can predict what we think will happen in a story. So far, each animal is trying to get the apples in a different way. Rabbit tried to jump but couldn't reach. Skunk tried to stand on Deer's back but couldn't reach. I think these animals are too little. I predict Deer will be able to get the apples because he is the biggest. Let's read on to see if my prediction is correct.

gap: space between

managed: did correctly

Make, Confirm, and Revise Predictions
Did Deer get the apples like we predicted? Who do you predict will get the apples now?

Text Structure: Sequence
What is the sequence in which the animals form the animal ladder? Who comes first? Who comes next? Which animal is the last?

The friends sat, thinking.

"The problem is they're too high," said Field Mouse.

"Or it might be that we're too low," said Deer.

"High-low, where do we go?" said Rabbit, who was a bit of a poet.

"Hmm," said Skunk. "High-low. How can we bridge the **gap**?"

"If only we had a ladder," said Rabbit.

"That's it!" cried Field Mouse. "WE can be the ladder! Deer, lean against the trunk. And bend your head."

Deer did just that.

"Now, Skunk, climb onto Deer's antlers."

Skunk did just that.

"I get it!" said Skunk. "I'll climb onto Deer's shoulders now."

Skunk stood on Deer's shoulders.

"My turn!" said Rabbit. And Rabbit **managed** to climb onto Skunk's shoulders.

Last, went Field Mouse, who climbed up Deer and Skunk and then climbed onto Rabbit.

Field Mouse stood on her tippy-tippy-toes and . . .Yes! She reached the apples! She scurried into the upper branches.

Plop! Plunk! Thunk!

Apples rained onto the ground.

Chomp! Munch! Crunch!

"Yay, Field Mouse!" the friends all called.

Everyone ate until their bellies were full.

"I'm not hungry anymore," said Rabbit.

"Is your stomach quiet like mine?" Skunk asked Field Mouse.

She patted her stomach. "You bet!"

"I have an idea," said Deer. And he began to **divide** the uneaten apples among the friends.

"Come visit for apple pie when the cold weather comes!" said Skunk.

"I can bring apple-sauce," said Deer.

"I can bring apple dumplings," said Rabbit.

"I can bring a growling tummy," said Field Mouse.

And all the animals laughed.

divide: make into smaller parts

Fantasy
How did the animals get the apples? What can you learn from them about solving problems?

Poetry

In poetry, words often rhyme. Which words rhyme in this stanza?

Ask and Answer Questions

Think Aloud

As we read, it helps to ask ourselves questions and to try and answer them. The words tell me that the grasshopper has legs like springs that help it do fantastic things. I ask myself why. Then I try to answer my own question. I know a spring can make something go up and down very fast. Then I picture the grasshopper's legs hopping up and down like a spring. That makes sense.

Hello, Grasshopper

Grasshopper, grasshopper—

Please don't stop.

I love to watch you hop, hop, hop!

Grasshopper, grasshopper—

Legs like springs

help you do fantastic things:

You hop straight up,

then hop so far.

You're an insect hopping star!

You hop through fields.

You hop through grass.

You hop through woods.

You hop down paths.

Singing as you hop along,

Your **cheerful**, buzzing summer song.

Grasshopper, grasshopper—

Lively bug,

I wish I could give you a great big hug!

cheerful: happy

lively: moves a lot, active

Key Details

Think Aloud

As we read, it helps to pay attention to key details in the pictures to understand the text better. When I look at the picture, I see how active, or lively, the grasshopper is by the way it is hopping. Also there are dotted lines that show all the places it has been. These details help me to understand how bouncy a grasshopper is!

If I Were a Butterfly

If I were a butterfly,
I'd spread out my wide wings.
I'd **flit** around the garden,
And visit lots of things:

I'd land upon a daisy,
and taste the nectar there.
I'd flutter to the rose bush
and smell the sweet, sweet air.

flit: move quickly
and lightly

Key Details

How does a butterfly spend its day? What key details help you know?

I'd **perch** upon the bird bath
To watch the world go by.
Then I'd **glide** across the field
And float up to the sky.

If I were a butterfly,
I'd fill my day with flight.
At sunset, I'd fold my wings
and rest throughout the night.

perch: sit on top of

glide: fly without flapping wings

Ask and Answer Questions
What questions do you have about the butterfly? Why do you think the girl wants to be a butterfly?

Poetry

What two words rhyme in the first stanza?

Key Details

Think Aloud

Remember that paying attention to key details can help us understand the text better. Here the poem talks about all kinds of buttons. Some buttons are round or square. Some have two holes. These are all key details that tell more about buttons. Let's pay attention to more key details about buttons as we read.

plain: simple; not a lot of extra parts

fancy: decorated with many things; not simple

Buttons

Buttons, buttons everywhere!

Some are round.

Some are square.

Two holes! Four holes!

Can you see three?

Blue buttons on you.

Red buttons on me!

Buttons, buttons!

Big and small.

Plain or **fancy**?

Let's sort them all!

Buttons here.

Buttons there.

Buttons on my teddy bear!

Little button eyes.

Big button nose.

Fancy buttons on

His teddy bear clothes.

Buttons, buttons everywhere!

Buttons round or buttons square?

Buttons green or buttons blue?

What kind of buttons

Are buttoned on you?

Key Details

Think Aloud

What kinds of buttons does the teddy bear have? Where are these buttons?

Little and Big

tossed: thrown

Ask and Answer Questions

Think Aloud

Remember, we can ask questions about things in the text we don't understand. I have read names of different things such as a peanut, a penny and a dollhouse chair. I ask myself why they are all together. I think about what they have in common. I think about the title of the poem, "Little and Big." Then I can answer my question. These are little things. As we read on, let's ask questions about things we don't understand.

A peanut, a penny, a dollhouse chair.
A pebble, a ball **tossed** up in the air.
One robin's egg, two shiny rings.
The world is full of LITTLE things.

3

The world is full of BIG things, too.
A fire truck, an elephant,
The sky so blue.

A Ferris wheel, a **skyscraper**,
A weeping willow tree.
So much of the world
Is bigger than me!

skyscraper: very tall building

Ask and Answer Questions
What questions do you have about this poem?

Informational Text

What are the five senses?

Key Details

Think Aloud

As I read, I pay attention to details to learn more. Here I read that when you look at something, you see shapes and sizes. You see colors and movement. These details help me to understand what I am looking at. I will think about shape, size, color, and movement when I try to describe what I see.

provides: gives

gain: get

describe: tell about something

My Senses

How can you learn about the world around you? One of the best ways is through your senses. You have five senses: seeing, hearing, smelling, touching, and tasting. Each sense **provides** a special kind of information.

Seeing

You use your eyes to see. What do you see when you look at something? You can see shapes and sizes. You can also see colors and movement. Imagine you see a tree. You know if its a big or small tree. You know that the leaves are green and that they are shaped a certain way. You can see how its branches in the wind. You can **gain** a lot of information from looking. Look at something in your classroom. **Describe** it exactly as you see it.

Smelling

You use your nose to smell. Most things have some kind of smell. Close your eyes. What kinds of smells can you notice in your classroom? Crayons have a smell. Books have a smell. How would you describe the way they smell? What does rain smell like? What do baking cookies smell like? What smells do you like?

Tasting

You taste with your tongue. There are almost as many **flavors** as there are foods. Otherwise we would just eat the same food for breakfast, lunch, and dinner. While all foods have their own special flavors, there are only five basic tastes. Sweet and salty are the most **common** tastes. Can you think of foods that taste sweet? Can you think of foods that taste salty? Another basic taste is sour. Look at the photograph of the boy tasting a lemon. That tastes sour! Which is your favorite taste?

flavors: tastes

common: usual or everyday

Ask and Answer Questions

Think Aloud

As I read, I ask myself questions to help me understand the text better. I learn that sweet and salty are the most common tastes. I ask myself what foods taste sweet or salty. I will continue to ask myself questions as I read.

Hearing

We hear with our ears. Sounds are everywhere. It is easy to notice loud sounds, like thunder or a honking car horn. But there are also many quiet sounds like a cat purring or raindrops falling. What quiet sounds can you think of?

Rumble, squeak, thump. These are all words that name sounds. A truck may rumble. A door being opened may squeak. A falling book may thump. Can you think of other things that sound like each of these words? What sound does a bell make? What sound does a slamming door make? What sound does a bumblebee make? Close your eyes. What sounds do you hear in your classroom?

Key Details
What are two different kinds of sounds?

Touching

You touch with your fingers, but you can feel things with all parts of your body. *Sticky, soft, smooth, rough, sharp.* All of these words describe the way things can feel. Glue feels sticky. Can you think of something else that is sticky? A feather is soft. Can you think of something else that feels soft? What does a marble feel like? How does sand feel? Which is smoother? Which is rougher?

Look at a Sense Scene

Look at the illustration of the park. There are many things to see, smell, hear, touch, and taste. What are they? How would you describe the way they look, smell, feel, sound, or taste?

Ask and Answer Questions

What questions do you have about the five senses?

Look and Learn

Nature is all around us. It is fun to observe nature, but you need the right tools.

What can you use? You can use your eyes!

We can see a lot with our eyes. We can see the color of a bird's feathers across the pond. We can see the ridges on the bark of a tree. We can see the colorful petals of a flower in the spring.

But there is a lot more to observe that we can't see. And there are tools that can help us observe nature.

Look! There is a furry caterpillar on a leaf. You want to get a closer look.

What can you use? A magnifying glass!

A magnifying glass makes tiny things look clearer and bigger. It can help you see small, crawly creatures like caterpillar or an **unusual** leaf. With a magnifying glass, you can see all the parts of a caterpillar.

unusual: doesn't happen often

Key Details

Think Aloud

As we read, we pay attention to key details in the text and photographs to learn more. I read that a magnifyng glass makes small things look bigger. I see the boy holding the magnifying glass close to a caterpillar. This helps me know that he is seeing the caterpillar as bigger than it is.

Rossario/Shutterstock.com

94   Informational Text

How does a magnifiying glass work? The lens bends light. This makes things look bigger. The first magnifying glasses were made thousands of years ago. They were used to make letters bigger for reading. Today, some people still use magnifying glasses to help them read.

Look! There are baby birds in a nest. You want to know what is happening in the nest. But it is in a high branch. It is too far away for you to see without a tool.

What can you use? Binoculars!

Binoculars help you see things that are far away. They use lenses that make things **appear** bigger. When you look through a pair of binoculars, the lenses help faraway things look much closer.

Raccoons and other interesting animals only come out at night. How could you observe them? You could use "night" binoculars. Night binoculars have special lenses that let you see what is happening in the dark!

Informational Text
How do you use binoculars? What do they look like? Describe them using the photograph.

Ask and Answer Questions

Think Aloud

When we read, it helps to ask ourselves questions. I read here that binoculars can help you see a baby bird in a high branch. I ask myself how this can happen. As I read on, I learn that the lens makes faraway things look closer.

appear: look or seem

Key Details

Key details in photographs can help us to understand the text. Look at the photograph. How do goggles help you see underwater?

clearly: easy to see

3

Look! There is a fish swimming in the water. You want to see what is happening under the water.

What can you use? Goggles!

Goggles help you see things **clearly** underwater. If you open your eyes underwater, things look blurry. But when you put on goggles, things are clear! Goggles keep the water out of your eyes. This makes everything more clear. You can see the beautiful colors and patterns on a fish that is deep in the water.

Look! There is the Moon. It has shadows and dark spots. You want to get a closer look.

What can you use? A telescope!

Telescopes make things that are really far away look bigger, closer, and brighter. Scientists use telescopes to study **distant** objects in the night sky. Like binoculars, telescopes use lenses to make things appear larger.

A long time ago, people didn't know what the stars were. But telescopes **solved** the mystery. Now, we know that stars are like our Sun.

All of the different tools can help you observe nature. But you may want to remember the things you have learned about your world.

What can you use? A pencil and notebook!

You can use a pencil to write down all you learned about nature in your notebook. You can draw pictures of what you saw. It's good to keep a record of nature. Share what you learned with your friends! And keep observing. Now you know what tools you can use!

distant: far away

solved: answered

Ask and Answer Questions

What questions do you have about the tools in this selection?

Genre

Informational Text
Informational text uses text and pictures to give information. Labels tell you what the pictures show.

Key Details

(Think Aloud)

I will pay attention to key details to help me guess each object. The text says that the object is a rectangle. It also says that you sleep in it. I know you sleep in a bed. A bed is also the shape of a rectangle. So I guess that the object is a bed. Paying attention to these key details helped me to guess the object. As we read, let's continue to pay attention to key details to help us guess the object.

leap: jump

Informational Text
What do the labels tell you about the picture?

Shapes All Day

Shapes are everywhere. You eat them, you sit on them, you ride in them, and you play with them.

Look at the shapes of the objects in the picture below. Can you name the shapes? Can you name more things that are that shape?

Now, listen to a story. The shape clues will help you to guess the object.

Shape Story

It is morning. An alarm goes off. You look at a circle with numbers on it to tell you the time. This circle is called a _____. (clock)

Next, you **leap** out of the rectangle you have been sleeping in. It's soft and has your favorite stuffed animals on it. This rectangle is called a _____. (bed)

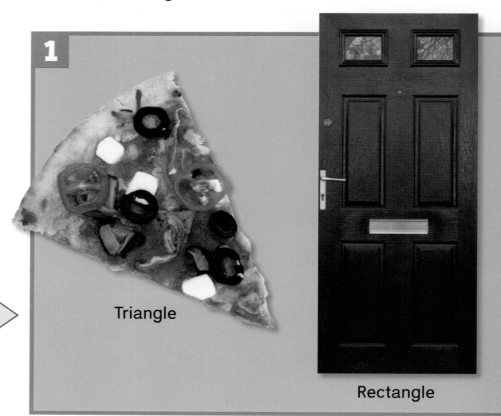

1

Triangle

Rectangle

You **gaze** out the window and see a yellow **circle** in the sky. No rain today! This circle is called the _____. (sun)

Now, it's time to get dressed. You **remove** a triangle from the closet. It has your favorite shirt on it. This triangle is called a _____. (hanger)

It's time to eat! Your dad is at the stove flipping a brown circle in the air. He asks if you want syrup on it. You say "Yes, of course!" This tasty breakfast food is called a_____. (pancake)

On the way out the door, your mom **offers** you a paper square. She tells you to use it to wipe your face. This paper square is called a _____. (napkin)

You wait with your dad for a yellow rectangle with four circles underneath. It will bring you to school. This rectangle with circles underneath is called a _____. (bus)

Square

Circle

(l)szefei/Shutterstock.com; (r)Ken Karp/McGraw-Hill Education

You get to school early. There is time to play in the playground! You run to a big square with sand in it. You sit inside and start to make a castle. This square is called a _____ . (sandbox)

It's time for school to begin. Your teacher **invites** you to sit on a circle on the floor. The circle is fuzzy and has lots of colors. This circle is called a _____ . (rug)

Syoza Hamal/EyeEm/Getty Images

invites: asks

Key Details
What triangles do you see in the photograph? What makes each of them a triangle?

2

Your teacher holds up a rectangle that has words and pictures. She turns the page and starts to read. This rectangle is called a _____. (book)

The story is about shapes.

Your teacher asks, "What shapes do you see every day?"

What is your answer?

Now, look at the photograph of the playground. There are circles, triangles, squares, and rectangles. What shapes do you see?

Ask and Answer Questions
What questions do you have about shapes?

Genre

Informational Text: Informational text can tell about things real people do.

Tools That Work!

Do you want to learn how to use tools? Guess what? You already know how to use lots of tools. You may even be using a tool now. There are all kinds of tools. People use special tools to help them do their jobs.

You have a job. It's to be a student. Your job at school is to learn. What tools do you use to help you to do that? Look around your classroom and you will see! Do you see books and magazines? These tools help to give you information. Do you see blocks and puzzles? These tools help you to learn how things are built and how to solve problems. Do you want to make a picture? There are probably lots of tools in your classroom that will help you.

Every job requires special tools. What tools would you get to use if you had another job? Let's find out!

Ask and Answer Questions

Think Aloud

When we read, it helps to ask ourselves questions about things we don't understand. The text says that I may be using a tool now! I ask myself what that means. I am not using a tool. I read on and I find out that there are lots of tools, and every job has tools. I am a teacher. What tool do you think I am using? Let's continue to ask questions and try to answer them as we read.

SerrNovik/iStock/Getty Images

2

A doctor's job is to keep people healthy. You've probably noticed some of the tools doctors use to **examine** your body. Doctors have different tools for examing different parts of you!

First, the doctor will check how you're growing by measuring your height and weight on a tool called a doctor's scale. It looks different from a scale at home!

Next, the doctor checks your body temperature with an electronic thermometer. These thermometers go in your mouth or ear and beep when they've measured your temperature. If your temperature is higher than normal, you have a fever.

Look at the picture. Do you know what this tool is called? It is a stethoscope. Doctors use it to listen to your heartbeats and breathing.

Does your doctor ask you to open your mouth wide and say "ahhh"? She is about to check your throat. She holds your tongue down with a tool that looks like a craft stick. Then she shines a special light to see if you have a sore throat. These are just some tools a doctor uses. Can you think of others?

examine: check

Key Details

Think Aloud

When we read , it helps to pay attention to key details that tell more about the topic. Here the text says that doctors use different tools for examining different things. That makes sense. As we read, let's think about how each tool helps to keep different parts of the body healthy.

Informational Text
Informational text can tell about what real people do. What does a doctor do make sure you are healthy?

Fuse/Corbis/Getty Images

expert: can do very well

ingredients: the different foods you use to make a dish

Key Details

Key details are important facts that help you understand the text. What tools help a chef chop and cut food?

grate: cut into very small pieces

What is your favorite dish? Macaroni and cheese? Apple pie? Whatever it is, someone used lots of special tools to make it. These are tools for making food. A professional cook, or a chef, is an **expert** at using them.

Chefs need tools for measuring **ingredients**. Measuring cups and spoons help them know how much flour and sugar to put in the pie crust or how much salt or rice to put in the soup. Measuring is a very important part of cooking. What would happen if you used too much salt in a soup?

What else do chefs need to do their job? They need tools for cutting and chopping. Knives help to chop apples for the pie or carrots for the soup. Blenders and food processors make the job easier. Spoons help to stir the ingredients so they all blend together. Some foods have their own special tools. If you are making a pie crust, you might use a rolling pin. If you want to **grate** cheese, you might use a cheese grater.

All kinds of tools are used to help make your meals!

Carpenters work with wood. They can make furniture. Chairs and tables and shelves are often made of wood. They can also make a whole house using wood. What else do they need? Tools!

Wooden furniture starts with small pieces of wood. Like chefs, the first things carpenters do is measure. Chefs use measuring cups. Carpenters use rulers to tell them how long and wide a wooden board should be. Otherwise, the shelves or tabletops might be too tall or too little or so **lopsided** that things would fall off!

Then they have to cut the boards to make them the right size. Chefs use knives to cut food. Carpenters use saws to cut wood. Next, the carpenters use hammers and nails to attach the boards. All of the tools carpenters use help make the furniture strong and beautiful.

Without tools to help us, our jobs would be much harder and much less fun!

Ask and Answer Questions
What questions do you have about how carpenters use tools to make furniture?

lopsided: uneven

Ask and Answer Questions

Think Aloud

Remember, we can ask ourselves questions if we are confused by what we read. Here the text says that long ago many people just threw things on the road without thinking about it. Today, we are always told to use trash cans. I ask myself how this changed. As we read on, let's try to answer this question.

billboards: very big signs on the road

views: what you can see from where you are

Lady Bird Cleans Up

Do you know what a litterbug is? It might sound like a fun thing to be. But it's not. Long ago, when your parents and grandparents were little, America was messier than it is today. Especially the roads and highways. People drove in cars and just threw their trash out the window. That was littering. Bottles, cans, and other trash littered the roads. Someone who threw trash away like that was called a litterbug!

Litterbugs were everywhere! Why? It wasn't because people *wanted* our roads to be ugly. In those days, people just didn't think about how throwing trash on the ground made the world less beautiful. And trash wasn't the only thing making our roads ugly. **Billboards** blocked **views** of mountains and other pretty scenery.

1

David Cupp/Denver Post/Getty Images

It took a special person to change all that. Her name was Claudia. But everyone called her Lady Bird. Lady Bird grew up in East Texas with her father and aunt. As a child, Lady Bird enjoyed being outdoors in nature more than anything. She loved exploring the woods and paddling her canoe, surrounded by plants and trees. But perhaps her favorite part of nature was the fields of wildflowers. She especially loved bluebonnets, the Texas state flower. She said they brought **joy** to her heart. Lady Bird would later say, "Where flowers bloom, so does hope."

Lady Bird grew up and married Lyndon Baines Johnson. In 1963, Lyndon became the president of the United States. And Lady Bird became the first lady.

Every first lady chooses a project to work on. This project is always something that will **benefit** the country.

joy: happiness

benefit: help

Ask and Answer Questions

What questions do you have about what Lady Bird will do as first lady? Think about the litterbugs and dirty highways you just read about. How can this help you to answer the questions?

laws: rules made by city or town or country

LBJ Library photo by Yoichi Okamoto

Text Structure: Sequence

Think Aloud

When we read, it helps to pay attention to sequence or what happens first, next, and last. Here I read that the first thing Lady Bird did was to decide to clean up the roads. Next, she worked with people to find the best way to clean up the roads. Words like first *and* next *help me to know the order in which these things happened. I wonder what she did next to help clean up the roads.*

Lady Bird wondered, *What should I do? What do I care about? What could help America?*

She remembered the days she spent in nature as a child. She thought about the wildflowers she loved. She believed they could also bring that joy to others. But how could she make that happen? She went to work.

First, she decided it was time to clean up those ugly highways and make our roadsides beautiful.

Next, she worked with many people to find the best ways to clean up America's highways. Some of these people worked on making new **laws** that said we had to work on cleaning up our highways. The law was called the Highway Beautification Act. It was made into law in 1965. Lady Bird was there when Lyndon Johnson signed the new law.

Then, people went to work cleaning up. Trash was removed. Billboards were taken down.

After that, grass and trees were planted. Workers also planted native wildflowers along many of the roads.

Last, people were urged *not* to throw trash out of their car windows. People learned why being a litterbug was harmful.

"Keep America Beautiful!" and "Don't be a litterbug!" became popular sayings. And it worked! Now, it is very rare to see someone throw trash out their window.

Now, adults and children traveling on our highways can enjoy the views of our country once again. They can enjoy the wildflowers by the roadside. All it took was a remarkable first lady and many others who pitched in and helped.

Text Structure: Sequence
What was the last thing workers did to help make the highways more beautiful?

Informational Text:
How did Lady Bird help to clean up the highways?

Firefighters Help Out!

Weeo-weeo-weeo! The fire truck's siren blasts up the street. The long, red truck comes rushing by, its red and white lights flashing. There's an emergency in the neighborhood, and the firefighters on board the truck are coming to the rescue!

Firefighters are some of the most important helpers in a community. When someone is in trouble, from a broken arm to a building on fire, firefighters are ready to help make things right. But even when there are no emergencies, firefighters stay busy.

What exactly does a firefighter do at work? Let's follow some firefighters for a day and find out!

Informational Text
Who is this selection about? What important things do they do?

blurAZ/Shutterstock.com

First, the firefighters arrive at the fire station in the morning, just in time to make a **hearty** breakfast. Yum! Next, the firefighters may check their fire engines and other equipment to be sure nothing is broken. They need to know that the water pumps and hoses are working, in case they have to put out a fire that day. Then the firefighters clean up the station. Yes, even firefighters have to sweep and wash dishes!

After they exercise, the firefighters might do some practice drills to help them remember how to act in different kinds of emergencies. Next, when all the chores are done, the firefighters get their **assignments** for the day. Maybe they will give a talk at a school to teach children about fire safety. Do you know how to *stop, drop, and roll?* The firefighters will teach you!

After that, the firefighters may go and **inspect** buildings to make sure they are safe for people if a fire breaks out. They check the exits and fire extinguishers in the buildings. They look at the fire safety plans the building has and make sure the plans will help people act wisely in an emergency.

hearty: a lot of food, filling

assignments: jobs to do

inspect: check to see if everything is good

Text Structure: Sequence

Think Aloud

When we read, it helps to think about the sequence, or order in which events happen. Words like first, next, after, *and* last *tell about sequence. I am reading about how firefighters spend their day. First they come to work and make breakfast. Next, they check their equipment. As we read, let's pay attention to the order in which the firefighters do things.*

emergency: a dangerous situation

thoroughly: carefully and completely

Sequence
What is the first thing firefighters do when they here the alarm?

Visualize

When we read it helps to visualize what the text is saying. Here it says the firefighters drop everything and whip into action. These words tell me how fast the firefighters need to go after the alarm. There is not time to put things away. They just put down what they have and get going!

Of course, if there is a real **emergency** at any time during their day, the firefighters drop everything and whip into action!

First the alarm goes off. Then they rush to the fire engine. They may slide down the fire pole to save time. Next, they put on their uniforms, they grab the hoses and place them on the truck, and jump in. Last, they sound the siren. *Weeo-weeo-weeo!* They're off!

Soon the firefighters are at the fire. Out come the hoses. If there is a fire hydrant nearby, firefighters will attach the hoses and water will spray out.

But wait! Someone may be stuck in the building. Firefighters have to check. They put on masks and special suits and enter. They may have to use an axe to knock down a door. They check the building **thoroughly** just in case.

After the fire is out, firefighters head back to the station. Now they drive at a normal speed and there is no siren. Even though the excitement is past, their day may not be over. Perhaps it is time for lunch. They may do some exercise. Firefighters need to stay in shape. It takes a lot of muscle to carry all that heavy equipment! No matter what time of day it is, firefighters keep busy.

More than anything, they care about keeping their community safe. Day and night, firefighters are ready to help out!

Visualize

How do you visualize the firefighters as they drive home from the fire? How are they different than they were on the way to the fire?

Main Topic and Key Details

Think Aloud

The main topic is what a text is mostly about. The first part of the text talks about how there are many kinds of trees. It says that each tree is different. I think this is the main topic. The text then says it will tell about the special features of four trees. I think these features will be the key details. Let's pay attention to these key details as we read.

features: special parts of something

All Kinds of Trees

Trees, trees, trees! Trees grow almost everywhere. They usually have a tall, woody trunk with branches coming out of it. They have roots that grow down into the ground. But just like you and your friends, trees don't all look alike. There are all kinds of trees. Each kind of tree is special and has unique **features**. Let's read about four trees and their special features.

Do you like to eat apples? Crunch! Apples are delicious. But apples don't appear on apple trees right away. An apple tree must grow for two or three years before it can start producing its yummy fruit. How does an apple tree grow? When you finish eating an apple, you can find the seeds in its core. Each small brown seed is the start of one apple tree. You can plant an apple seed in the ground. If you give it water and let the sun warm it soon, a little green sprout will pop up out of the earth.

Over time, this sprout becomes a hard, woody trunk with leafy branches. In spring, the tree grows pretty pink or white blossoms. When the blossoms fall off, apples begin to grow. The delicious fruits and pretty blossoms make apple trees very popular.

The rainbow eucalyptus tree is special because of the colorful stripes on its trunk and branches. It looks like someone painted this tree with bright colors, but it actually grows like this. The smooth bark of the rainbow eucalyptus peels away as it grows, and new bright green bark appears. As the new bright green bark gets older, it changes color to dark green, blue-purple, pink-orange, and reddish-brown: a whole rainbow of colors!

Reread

Think Aloud

If we come to something we don't understand, we can reread the text that came before. Here it says that apples begin to grow when the blossoms fall off. But its an apple tree. Aren't the apples always there? Let me go back and reread. I see that it said "an apple tree must grow for two or three years before it can start producing yummy fruit." Now I understand why it is just beginning to grow fruit.

Main Topic and Key Details

The main topic of this piece is what makes trees unique. What makes the giant sequoia special?

wide: the size from side-to-side

story: one floor in a building

Can you guess what makes the giant sequoia tree special? A word in its name is a clue. Giant sequoias are the largest kind of tree. Unlike most other trees, they can live for thousands of years. But just like other trees, the giant sequoia starts out as a seed that sprouts into a seedling.

Giant sequoias grow tall and **wide** quickly. The largest giant sequoia alive today weighs 642 tons. That's as heavy as 107 elephants! They can be as tall as a 26-**story** building!

Another giant tree is the baobab. Baobabs have no leaves most of the year. Their branches stick straight up in the air, so they look like the roots that grow out of the tree's bottom. That is why this strange-looking tree is sometimes called the Upside-Down Tree.

Another special feature of the baobab is the blossoming of its beautiful white flowers. If you want to see this **rare** and amazing sight, you need to climb way up to the top of the tree. And make sure you bring your flashlight—because these flowers **bloom** only at night!

There are thousands of different kinds of trees in the world. Just like people, trees have special features that make them unique. Sometimes, these special features take years to appear. And sometimes, they appear for just one day. What makes the trees you know special?

Jialiang Gao/Moment/Getty Images

Genre

Informational Text:
Informational text can tell about the sequence, or the order, in which things happen.

Reread

Think Aloud

When we come to something in the text we don't understand, it can help to go back and reread what comes before. At first, I don't understand why farmers plant seeds in a greenhouse instead of the ground. Then I reread the text that comes before and learn that farmers do this because the winter ground is frozen. That makes sense.

sprout: when a plant begins to grow

A Farm Year

Winter, spring, summer, fall—in each season, farmers have different jobs so they can grow food for us. What are those jobs? When do farmers do them? Let's follow the farmers through the seasons and find out!

It's busy on the farm all year. In winter, farmers sit around a big table and sort seeds. They need to choose the healthiest ones to plant. They want the seeds to grow into food, like beans, lettuce, corn, carrots, and berries.

After the farmers choose the best seeds to plant, they get busy planting them. But the winter ground is frozen and hard, so the farmers plant the seeds in a big, warm greenhouse. A greenhouse is like a house made of glass. The glass lets in lots of sunlight. In just a couple of weeks, the sun will help the seeds **sprout**. The farmers water the sprouts. Soon the greenhouse will be full of little green seedlings!

More weeks pass. The frozen winter ground starts to **thaw**. The temperature outside gets warmer. The farmers check their calendars. It's spring! It is time to move the seedlings from the greenhouse and replant them in the fields.

The first thing a farmer must do is to make sure the soil in the fields is ready for planting. That means breaking up the hard soil. Farmers can use tractors to help them.

Next, the farmers plant the seedlings in groups. One group will become a big pumpkin patch. Other groups of seedlings will become rows of crunchy carrots and tall stalks of corn.

All during spring, the farmers **tend** their crops. They water the fields. Then they pull up weeds to give the seedlings room to grow. The seedlings' roots push down into the soil. The stems sprout green leaves that soak up the sun. Days pass, and the seedlings become bigger and stronger!

thaw: warm up and soften

Informational Text

In spring, farmers move the seedlings from the greenhouse to the fields. What do the farmers do first? What do they do next?

tend: take care of

Main Topic and Key Details

When we read, it helps to think about the main topic, or what the text is mostly about. This selection is about what happens on a farm during each season. Here I read that in summer, farmers put up nets and fences to keep animals from eating their crops. This key detail tells more about the main topic . As we read, we will continue to look for key details that tell us more about the main topic.

.

Next, it is summer. The farmers must keep the plants growing and healthy. They make sure the plants have enough water in the hot summer sun. They keep away bugs. They put up nets and fences to keep animals from eating the new fruits and vegetables. They add special plant food to the soil to make it good for crops to grow.

During summer, many crops are ready to harvest. The farmers pick beans, berries, corn, and lettuce. They dig up carrots and potatoes. The pumpkin patch grows long vines of pumpkins. Some are as big as basketballs - or even bigger!

PobladuraFCG/iStock/Getty Images Plus

After summer comes fall. Now, all the fields are filled with delicious foods. The weather turns cool. The farmers need to pick the crops that might **freeze**. They sell corn and beans and lettuce at the farmers' market. They make jam with the berries and sell that, too. The farmers put up a big sign that says, 'Pick Your Own Pumpkin!' Families come searching for the biggest and best pumpkin to bring home.

When fall ends, winter returns. Soon, the farmers will sit around the big table again and sort seeds for planting. It's busy on the farm all year!

Main Topic and Key Details
The main topic of this section is what happens on a farm in the fall. What key details tell about what happens?

Reread:
Why do farmers sort seeds? What text could you reread to find out?

freeze: hurt by the cold

adorable: very cute

Reread

[Think Aloud]

If we come to something we don't understand, it can help to go back and reread the parts that come before. Here the text says that the cubs drink their mothers' milk until spring. But it doesn't say when they start drinking it. I will reread the paragraph. Let's see if we can answer this question. Oh, here it says that the cubs are born in winter. That means they drink the milk from winter until spring.

Dmitriy Kostylev/Shutterstock.com

Baby Animals Are Alike and Different!

Some are furry, some are feathered, some are wrinkled, some are rough—but one thing is the same—baby animals are all **adorable**! Think of baby animals you know. Do they seem the same? How are they not the same? Baby animals can be alike and different. Let's look at four kinds of baby animals and find out more.

First, let's start with names. Most baby animals have their own special names. What do you call a baby bear? A cub! Brown bear cubs are born in winter. They are tiny then, and only weigh around 1 pound. They can't see yet and they have no hair! But the cubs drink their mothers' milk until spring and grow fast. After that, they eat berries and nuts and leaves. The cubs live with their mothers for two and a half years. But after that, they prefer to live alone.

Informational Text
What does the picture tell you about the elephant calf? What information do you learn that is not in the text?

Did you know that brown bears climb trees? But only when they are cubs. These bears can weigh 1,000 pounds when they are grown. That's much too heavy for tree climbing!

What do you call a baby African elephant? A calf! Unlike a baby bear who weighs only a pound, elephant calves are very big babies. They weigh about 220 pounds when they're born! They drink their mothers' milk for longer than a bear cub does—from six months to a year and a half. Then they eat leaves, branches, fruit, grass, and bark.

A bear cub has its mom, but elephant calves live in a herd of female elephants. Everyone helps babysit—sisters, aunts, and cousins all help the mothers keep their calves safe. African elephant calves grow up to be the largest animals on land. But it's a lot of work to stay that big— elephants can spend 16 hours a day eating!

Text Structure: Compare and Contrast

Think Aloud

When we read, it helps to compare or think about how things are alike. The text says that elephant calves and bear cubs both drink their mothers' milk. That is one way they are alike. It also helps to contrast, or think about about how things are different. Here it says that bear cubs are only cared for by their moms. But elephant calves are cared for by lots of aunts and cousins, too.

3

Can you guess the name for a baby penguin? It's chick! Like other birds, penguin chicks hatch from an egg. Usually a penguin mom lays one or two eggs at a time. When the chicks are ready to hatch, they poke their way out of their eggs with their beaks. This might take a few days. Some chicks have very few feathers, so their parents protect them from the sun and cold by huddling close.

Unlike cubs and elephants who drink their mothers' milk, penguin chicks are fed real food by their parents. But the parents chew the food first to make sure it is soft enough for the baby penguin. They do this until chicks are big enough to hunt on their own. Penguins like to eat fish and other sea **creatures**. Most birds have wings for flying, but penguins can't fly at all. Instead, they have special flippers that help them swim to find food!

What is a baby alligator called? A hatchling! Like the penguin chick, it also hatches from an egg. Alligator mothers make a big nest on land. The mother covers the nest with leaves and mud to protect it.

creatures: living thing

Reread

Why do penguins have to swim to find food? Let's reread the part that came before to find out.

When the hatchlings are ready to be born, they make a high noise to **alert** their mother. The mother then **clears off** the covering of the nest and the hatchlings poke their way out of the eggs. They use a special tooth at the end of their nose called an "eye-tooth." Unlike a penguin, alligators are hatched with many, many brothers and sisters. Mothers can lay up to 50 or more eggs at one time. Hatchlings are weak, so their mothers need to protect them for a year.

As they grow, hatchlings enjoy eating snails, worms, insects, fish, and birds. Baby alligators may look **fierce**, but they still get scared. They make a special sound to call their mothers when they need help! It takes hatchlings two years to grow to be six feet long and become adults.

Cubs, calves, chicks, and hatchlings are all alike in some ways and different in others. One way they are the same is that all these babies will grow up to be adults—and soon they'll be the moms and dads of more baby animals just like them!

alert: let someone know what is happening

clears off: takes away

Text Structure: Compare and Contrast
How is the way baby alligators and baby penguins hatch the same? How is it different?

fierce: mean

NPSPhoto

Informational Text: Informational text can use text, photographs, and illustrations to give information about a topic.

Our Country Celebrates!

Do you like parades? How about fireworks? Or enjoying a delicious meal? These are all things people do to celebrate **national** holidays. But what *is* a national holiday? And why do we celebrate them? National holidays are special days that our country celebrates every year. We celebrate them to remember important people and events that helped to shape our country.

The first national holiday we celebrate each year is Martin Luther King Jr. Day, which happens on the third Monday every January. On this day, we celebrate the life of Dr. Martin Luther King Jr. Dr. King worked hard to make our country a fair place for everyone to live. He believed in freedom for all people. On this day, we watch and listen to recordings of Dr. King's famous speeches.

Main Topic and Key Details

Think Aloud

When we read informational text, it helps to think about the main topic or what the text is mostly about. Here the text says, What is a national holiday? And why do we celebrate them? *I think this is the main topic. The rest of the text will help answer these questions. These are the key details. As we read, let's pay attention to key details that tell us what national holidays are and how we celebrate them.*

national: about the whole country

Informational Text
What does this photograph tell about why we celebrate Martin Luther King Jr.?

1

(l)Courtesy National Gallery of Art, Washington, (r)Library of Congress, Prints and Photographs Division LC-USP6-2415-A1

honor: show that you like and respect

united: to act together

ceremonies: what we do to celebrate special times

To **honor** Dr. King, people like to help others in their community just as he did. They might help out by serving food to people who are hungry, or they might help children do homework at the library. Martin Luther King Jr. Day is a good day to remember that it's a great idea for all kinds of people to get along and care for one another.

About a month later, on the third Monday of every February, we celebrate another national holiday; President's Day. On this day we honor all the presidents of our country from long ago until today. We especially remember the lives of two famous U.S. presidents from our past: George Washington and Abraham Lincoln. Both these presidents helped America become a strong and **united** country. Schools are often closed on this day, and people hold public **ceremonies** where the U.S. president lives, in Washington, DC. President's Day used to be called Washington's Birthday, in celebration of George Washington's birthday. Later, the name was changed so more presidents could be honored. Happy Birthday to all of our presidents!

Reread

Think Aloud

Remember, we can reread if we come to something in the text we don't understand. Here it says that many peope choose to help help others as a way to honor Dr. King. I wonder why they do that. I will go back and read the part that came before. When I do, I see that the text says that Dr. King worked hard to make the country a fair place for everyone to live. That tells me why people want to help others to honor him.

independence:
freedom

Main Topic and Key Details

What details tell why we celebrate the Fourth of July?

A few months later, our country celebrates another special date—the Fourth of July! This national holiday is also called **Independence** Day, because it marks the day our country became a separate nation with its own president and government. Today, people can chose who they think can run the country best.

To celebrate, some businesses are closed on this day, and there are many parades in towns and cities. People enjoy picnicking in parks, and later, when it's dark, many places hold exciting fireworks displays. Boom! The sky explodes with colorful lights to remember the battles that helped America win the war for our independence.

Another important national holiday is Thanksgiving. A long time ago, a group of people known as pilgrims sailed across the Atlantic Ocean from a country called England. The people who lived where they landed, the Wampanoag, helped them to grow food.

We celebrate Thanksgiving to remember the first feast that was shared by the pilgrims and the Wamapanoag. On Thanksgiving, families and friends gather around dinner tables to eat many of the foods that were shared at the first Thanksgiving feast so long ago. We eat turkey, beans, corn, and pumpkin. On this day, we give thanks for everything we are glad for in our lives.

Celebrating national holidays is a way for the whole nation to share special memories. We remember the people and events that made our country great. National holidays are important, but they are also fun. The next time you celebrate a national holiday, think of all the other people in our country who are celebrating, too. National holidays bring people together, whether they are marching in parades, watching fireworks, or enjoying a feast. Let's celebrate!

Reread
Who were the pilgrims and the Wampanoag? Let's reread the first part of this section to help us remember.

kali9/E+/Getty Images

Genre

Informational Text: Informational text can have illustrations. The illustrations contain additional information about the topic.

Visualize

Think Aloud

Remember, we can visualize to help us understand the text better. This means to use the words to form a picture in our minds. Here the text tells me that some dinosuaurs were as long as garbage trucks. I try to visualize a dinosaur standing next to a garbage truck. This helps me understand how big it is. Let's continue to visualize as we read about these fascinating creatures.

creatures: animals or other living things

mighty: strong and powerful

attentive: caring

Dinosaurs Are Different!

Long, long ago, amazing **creatures** called dinosaurs lived on Earth. Some were as long as garbage trucks. Some had tails, and some had scales. Some had feathers; some had horns. Let's look at four dinosaurs and see how they are the same and how they are different.

The **mighty** Tyrannosaurus Rex, or T. Rex, is one of the most well-known dinosaurs. These dinosaurs were fierce. But scientists think they were actually **attentive** parents who took care of their young. People also believe that T. Rex was one of the largest meat-eating dinosaurs. T. Rex was a giant, around 40 feet long and 12 feet tall. That's about the size of a school bus.

T. Rex had very strong legs, a great big tail, and two claws at the end of each arm. Its large jaw was so mighty, it could crush bones while it ate. Crunch!

T. Rex ate other animals and dinosaurs, and its huge, sharp teeth could chew up to 500 pounds of food in one bite. This wild beast was enormous, but believe it or not, its arms were too short to reach its mouth!

In a different part of the world, Triceratops **roamed**. Triceratops got its name because *tri-* means three, and it had three horns on its face. It also had a big bony piece called a *frill* behind its head. Triceratops was about 30 feet long, a little smaller than the T. Rex. It had four strong legs and a heavy body. Its giant head was one of the biggest heads of all the animals that lived on land, and inside its powerful mouth were as many as 800 teeth! But unlike the T. Rex, Triceratops used its mighty teeth to munch on plants instead of meat. Triceratops was probably not a big fighter. Because of that, some people call this dinosaur "the gentle giant."

Informational Text
Look at the picture of the T. Rex and the picture of the Triceratops? How are they alike and different?

roamed: went freely, wandered

Text Structure: Compare and Contrast

Think Aloud

When we read informational text, it can help to compare and contrast information. This means to think about how things are the same and how they are different. I read that the Triceratops and T. Rex are alike because they both have powerful teeth and eat a lot. But they are different because Triceratops ate plants. The T. Rex ate a lot of meat.

recognize: see something familiar

Text Structure: Compare and Contrast

How are Stegosaurus and Triceratops alike? How are they different?

Stegosaurus is about the same size as Triceratops. But it did not have horns on its face. Instead, it had two rows of flat spikes that ran along the back of its neck all the way down to its tail. People think these spikes were a way for these dinosaurs to **recognize** one another.

Like Triceratops, Stegosaurus ate plants instead of meat. But unlike Triceratops, Stegosaurus did not have a powerful mouth. It had a beak and small, weak teeth.

Believe it or not, you can probably bite harder than Stegosaurus! Also, scientists think that the different lengths of this dinosaur's legs meant that it couldn't run very fast. If you could race a Stegosaurus, you just might win!

Apatosaurus was one of the largest animals that walked on land. This dinosaur was around 75 to 85 feet long. That is about as long as a big swimming pool or a tennis court. It is about twice the size of the mighty T. Rex.

Unlike T. Rex, Apatosaurus had a small head compared to its body. Most people recognize Apatosaurus by its extremely long neck and long, slim tail. Like Triceratops and Stegosaurus, Apatosaurus did not eat meat. Scientists believe this dinosaur had to eat almost 900 pounds of plants a day to survive. That's about as much as a polar bear weighs.

There are no dinosaurs alive today. We don't know everything about dinosaurs, but scientists are discovering more about them all the time. Dinosaurs may be different from each other, but one thing is the same—they are all amazing!

Visualize

Close your eyes and visualize the size of a big swimming pool. Then think of Apatosaurus being the same size. How else do you visualize this dinosaur?

Make It from Nature!

Look around you right now. You probably see things like clothes and books and furniture. Did you ever wonder what those things are made of? Many things we use every day are made from natural resources. What is a natural resource? It is something found in nature. For example, water, plants, animals, sand, and stone are all natural resources. We use natural resources to make the clothes we wear, the paper we write on, the furniture we sit on, and the cars we drive. In fact, most things we use started in nature. Sometimes in **unexpected** ways!

Trees are very important. They keep the air clean and help Earth stay healthy. Many animals need trees to survive. Trees are also important because that is where we get wood. And we need wood to make things!

unexpected:
surprising

Informational Text
What can you learn from this picture about how trees are made into wood?

People can use wood to make many different things. Paper, toys, furniture, and buildings are just some of the things you use every day that are made from wood. Let's find out more about how we get wood.

First, workers called lumberjacks chop down a tall tree. "Timberrrr!" they cry as the tree falls to the ground. That warns others to get out of the way.

Next, they drag the tree to a clear place. Then, the tree's leaves and branches are cut off. That leaves just the main trunk, or log. After many logs are cut, people load them onto a truck.

The truck will take the logs to a sawmill. At the sawmill, a machine peels the bark off the tree trunks to make the logs smoother. Then another big machine saws the logs into different-sized boards called lumber. Last, a truck will take the lumber to the lumberyard where customers can buy it.

What can people make with the lumber they buy? How about a beautiful chair? Or maybe a treehouse!

Text Structure: Sequence

Think Aloud

Thinking about sequence, or the order in which things happen, can help us understand a text better. Words like first, next, *and* last *tell about sequence. Here we are learning about how trees become wood. It says the first the tree gets chopped down. I will look for what happens next.*

3

Another important natural resource is metal. There are many kinds of metal, such as gold, silver, tin, copper, and iron. Metal is very strong, which means it's good for making things like bridges and buildings. Metal is also good for making tools, like hammers and nails.

You use metal a lot in your daily life. The fork you eat with is probably made of metal. Do you have toy trucks or feed your pet canned foods? Both toy trucks and canned foods are usually made of metal. Like wood, metal is found in nature. Let's find out more about how people get metal.

Dig! Dig! Dig! A big machine shovels the earth, hunting for metal. Most metal is found in special kinds of rocks. Often, these rocks are **located** far underground. First, people look for areas that **contain** a lot of these special rocks. They use machines to dig a long tunnel called a mine. Next, workers called miners go down into the tunnel to dig up the rocks containing metal. Then, the metal is loaded up and brought to the surface.

located: where something is found

contain: have in them

Sequence
What it the first thing that has to be done to get metal?

After that, the rocks are crushed. Sometimes, chemicals are added to help get the metal out of the rock. People may add water or they may heat the metal in order to get rid of any bits of dirt or rock in it. They want to make sure the metal is very **pure**.

After that, people use the metal to make all kinds of things. If it's something big like beams for a building, it will go to big factory. But if it's something small like a ring or special bowl, crafts people called metalsmiths might work with it. They use heat and special tools to shape the metal the way they want it. Look around you. What do you see that might be made of metal?

We are **fortunate** to have so many natural resources on our planet. Natural resources are nature's gift to people. And as long as we use these resources responsibly, people will be able to keep making useful things from nature for many years to come.

4

Reread

Think Aloud

Remember, we can reread if we come to something that we don't understand. I wonder why they need to get the metal out of rocks. I will go back and reread the part that came before. There it says, Most metal is found in special kinds of rocks. *Now I understand why.*

Reread

What natural resources do we need to protect? Let's go back to the first part of the selection and reread to find out.

pure: very clean

fortunate: lucky

Lutai Razvan/EyeEm/EyeEm Premium/Getty Images

Informational Text

What details tell you how water is used by animals and people?

Main Topic and Key Details

Think Aloud

When we read, it can help to think about the main topic or what the selection is mostly about. I read this sentence, "Let's find out more about water and why it is so important to protect it." Now I understand that this is what the text will mostly be about. As we read on, let's look for key details that tell more about protecting water.

gulp: drink quickly

valuable: important, worth a lot

Watch That Water!

Ducks splash it, elephants squirt it, and people **gulp** it on a hot day. What is it? Water! All living things use water. From tiny plants to enormous whales, every living thing needs water to stay alive.

Your family uses a lot of water every day, too. Besides drinking it, people use water for bathing, cooking, cleaning, growing food, and putting out fires. People use water to have fun when they swim, ice skate, and sail.

Water is one of our most **valuable** natural resources. A natural resource is something found in nature that can be used by people. Let's find out more about water and why it is so important to protect it.

1

Multistock/Shutterstock.com

2

Did you know that almost all of our planet's **surface** is water? Look at the picture of Earth. Do you see a lot of blue? That shows where water is found.

Most of Earth's water is in the ocean. Ocean water is too salty for people and most animals and plants to drink. A small amount of water is frozen in ice caps at the North and South Poles, so we can't use that water, either.

That leaves only a tiny bit of Earth's water for people and other living things to use, and some of this water is too dirty for people to safely drink.

There is still enough water to go around, but we need to take care of the water we have.

How do we do that?

surface: the top part or cover

Reread

(Think Aloud)

Here it says that only a tiny bit of Earth's water can be used. I am not sure why. Let's reread the parts that came before to help me understand. When I reread, it says that ocean water is too salty to drink. That helps to explain it. Let's continue to reread if we come to something we don't understand.

supply: how much you have of something needed

simple: very easy

Main Topic and Key Details

What are some things you can do to help save water?

There are many ways that people can protect our water **supply**. You can save a lot of water every day, just by doing these three **simple** things.

1. Whenever you wash your hands, wet them, and then turn the water off. Rub your hands with soap, then turn the water on to rinse.

2. Don't let the water run while you brush your teeth or wash your face.

3. Remember, when you turn off the water, make sure nothing drips out. If you see a faucet dripping, tell an adult right away. Even little drips can waste a lot of water!

Here are some other ways to save water.

Which uses less water, a shower or a bath? If you guessed a shower, you're right! One way to save water is to take a five-minute shower instead of a bath. This can save many gallons of water.

Another way to use water **wisely** is to save the water that is used to prepare meals and wash fruits and vegetables. You can collect this water and give it to your thirsty houseplants.

Speaking of thirsty, if you like cold water, don't run the faucet waiting for water to get cold. Just keep a pitcher of water in the refrigerator.

All living things need water to survive. We must be careful to protect it so we always have enough.

Now you know a lot of ways to save this valuable natural resource. You can share these water-saving tips with your friends and family. Tell them that we need to share Earth's water with every living creature. Remind them that it's up to all of us to watch that water!

wisely: thoughtfully

Reread
Why is it so important to save water? Let's reread the beginning to help us remember.